Essential Piano Keyboard Technique

- ✦ Early-intermediate to advanced levels
- ✦ Exceeds state and national guidelines

Barry Michael Wehrli

Essential Piano and Keyboard Technique

 The letter C with a circle around it stands for the word **copyright**.

Copyright is made up of two words:
Copy: To make a picture of or create another of something.
Right: Permission to own, create or use something.

The copyright on this book protects the rights of its publisher to copy, sell, give away, make changes in, or publicly show the book to others. To do so without the publisher's written permission violates the publisher's rights.

The **copyright notice** is the copyright symbol, the date of publication, and the name of the publisher, as shown at the top of this page.

Wehrli Publications

Cutting-Edge Books and Products
for the Music Teacher and Retailer

12830 Burbank Boulevard, Box 204, Valley Village, CA 91607-1402 www.wehrlipubs.com

Cover designed by Sandy Fox, eMedia Solutions, Inc.

Foreword

Essential Piano and Keyboard Technique is a thorough and comprehensive study of keyboard technique, taking early-intermediate students well into advanced levels.

Four sections present technical exercises by type or category for easy reference.

This book follows current technical guidelines established by the California Association of Professional Music Teachers (CAPMT) and the Music Teachers' Association of California (MTAC).

Concise tips on basic posture, practice techniques and strategies are presented in **Piano Practice and Performance**, available at wehrlipubs.com, amazon.com and select retailers.

About the Author

Barry Michael Wehrli began piano and keyboard studies at the age of eight. His formal training includes instruction from Dolores Rhoads, Terry Trotter and John Novello and music studies at California State University, Northridge. He composes, arranges and records at his home studio, is a freelance performer, heads Wehrli Publications and teaches piano and electronic music. His clients include Warner Brothers, Yamaha, and local professional musicians and teachers.

Many Thanks

To my parents and teachers for nurturing and cultivating my love of music.
To my wonderful wife for her valuable assistance in creating this book.

How to use this Book

- A piano or touch-sensitive (dynamic) 88-key instrument with a damper pedal is required.

- Guidance by a competent piano instructor is recommended.

- A workable, consistent practice schedule is required.

- Terms presented in this book can be found in any music dictionary.

- A checksheet begins each of the four sections, introducing its topic(s) and project list. The box next to each project is checked off by the instructor or self-study student when completed in its presented form. "Supplemental" exercises are suggested, but not required.

- Each project, once started, is to be completed in full. This means played with correct posture, at or above the suggested tempo range and without error.

- Study sequence depends on three factors:
  1. Relevance, meaning one technique building upon another. Major scales followed by blocked and broken major triads, followed by hand over hand major triads, is one possible sequence.
  2. Specific goals.
  3. Specific weaknesses.

- Section 1 exercises should be transposed to as many different keys as possible. The Major and Minor 5-Finger Patterns on page 3 may be used as a template for playing selected exercises in different positions or keys. Students not yet familiar with sharps, flats or naturals should still transpose exercises into different positions, visualizing the pattern of half and whole steps on the keyboard rather than reading the notation of the Major and Minor 5-Finger Patterns.

- Dynamic and/or articulative variation should eventually be applied to all technique, both in this book and beyond. The 5-Finger Articulations on pages 6-10 present many useful ways to vary articulation. The four dynamic sets shown on page 5 develop dynamic control. This kind of variety keeps technique interesting and musical over the many years it is to be maintained.

- Technique should be played hands separately, even if an exercise is easy enough to begin hands together. When listening to and observing each hand, mechanical problems become more noticeable. Rhythmic precision is also heightened when a syncopated hand is played alone against the beat. In some cases the hands are not meant to be joined, as in the hand jump exercises beginning on page 13. Cadences and chord progressions should be studied hands separately, then together.

- Mastery at the *suggested* tempo range should be considered a "first-stage" accomplishment which allows the student to begin other studies. As these exercises are maintained over time, speed is gradually increased.

- Depending on the exercise, range should also be increased over time. For example, though the scales in this book are presented in two octaves as eighth notes, they are eventually played in four octaves as sixteenth notes, and at ever-increasing tempos. (Advanced versions are easily extrapolated from the various scale activities presented here.)

Essential Piano and Keyboard Technique

Table of Contents

Essential Piano and Keyboard Technique

Section 1 Checksheet

General Technique

✓	**PROJECTS**
☐	Major and Minor 5-Finger Patterns
☐	5-Finger Articulations #1 - 5
☐	5-Finger Articulations #6 - 10
☐	5-Finger Articulations #11 - 15
☐	5-Finger Articulations #16 - 20
☐	5-Finger Articulations #21 - 28
☐	Finger Switching #1 - 8
☐	Hand Jumps #1 - 8
☐	Hand Jumps #9 - 16
☐	Wrist Rotation #1 - 8
☐	Trills #1 - 2
☐	Trills #3 - 4
☐	Tremolos #1 - 4
☐	Wrist Strokes #1 - 4
☐	Repeated Notes #1 - 8
☐	Finger Independence #1 - 12
☐	Finger Independence #13 - 20
☐	Finger Independence #21 - 23
☐	Thirds #1 - 8
☐	Hand Over Hand - One Hand Static #1 - 2
☐	Wrist Turning #1 - 12

Major and Minor 5-Finger Patterns

M.M. = 66 - 84

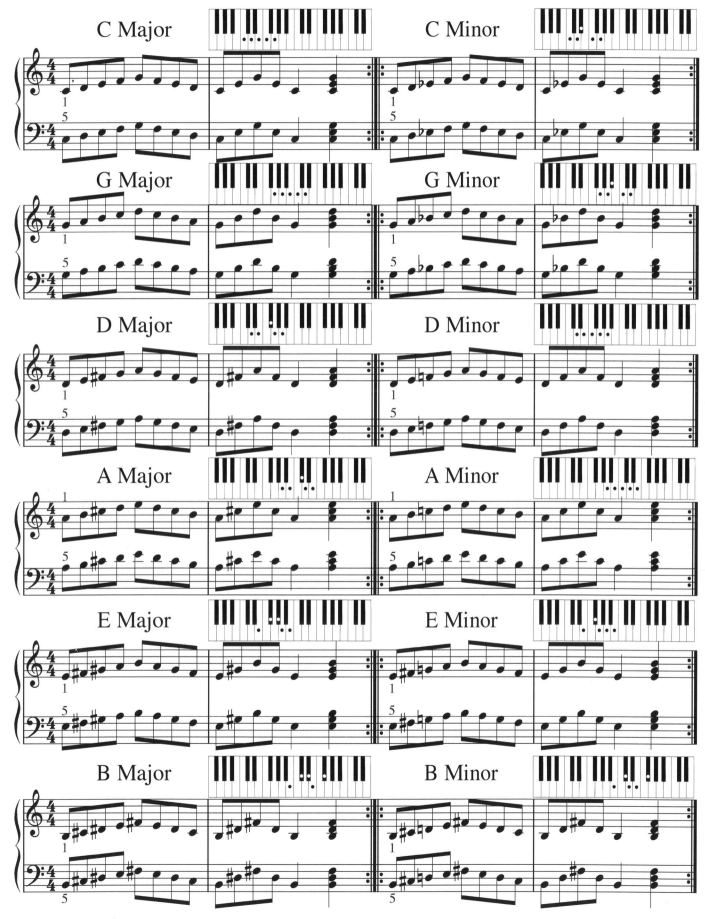

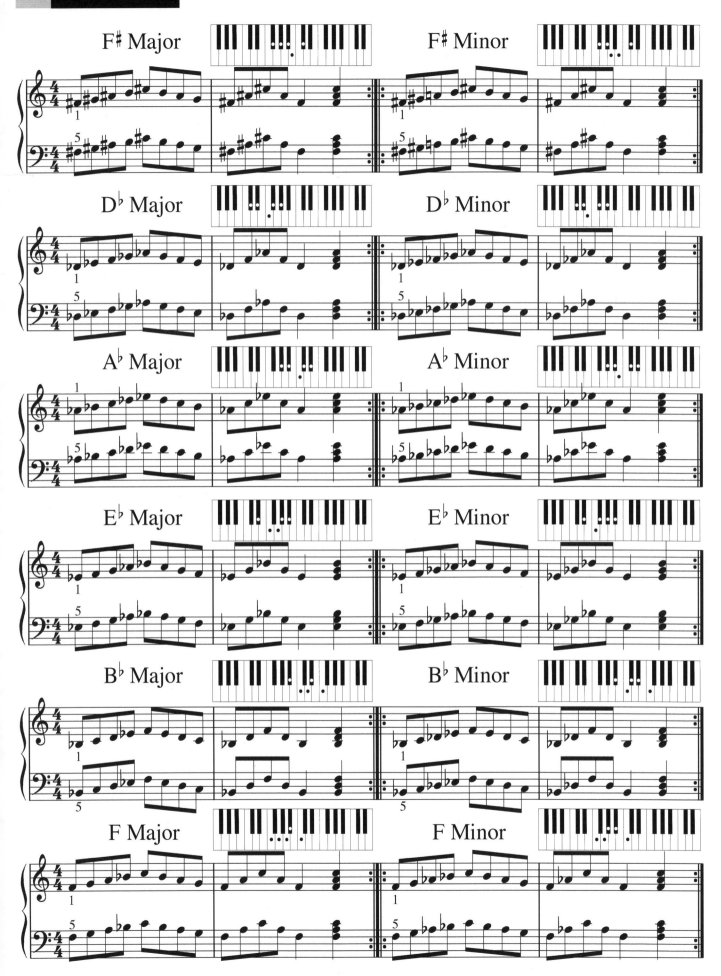

Regimen for the 5-Finger Articulations

The 5-Finger Articulations are designed to produce a masterful touch at the keyboard.
Once each exercise is learned at a slow and steady tempo, the four dynamic sets are mastered
in the sequence shown below and speed is gradually increased to the suggested tempo range.

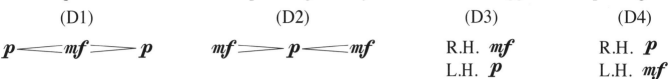

The first articulation exercise is reproduced below with its dynamic sets D1, D2, D3 and D4,
as an example. Memorize this regimen, as these dynamic sets are not printed for each exercise.
Learning each exercise in a new major and/or minor key is highly recommended.

5-Finger Articulations
Alternating Hands in Contrary Motion - R.H. Leads

M.M. = 72 - 92 Play 4 times, then end.   Practice L.H. alone for rhythmic accuracy.

Alternating Hands in Contrary Motion - L.H. Leads

M.M. = 72 - 92 Play 4 times, then end.   Practice R.H. alone for rhythmic accuracy.

Alternating Hands in Parallel Motion - R.H. Leads

M.M. = 72 - 92 Play 4 times, then end.

Alternating Hands in Parallel Motion - L.H. Leads

M.M. = 72 - 92   Play 4 times, then end.

Simultaneous Hands in Parallel Motion

M.M. = 72 - 92   Play 8 times, then end.

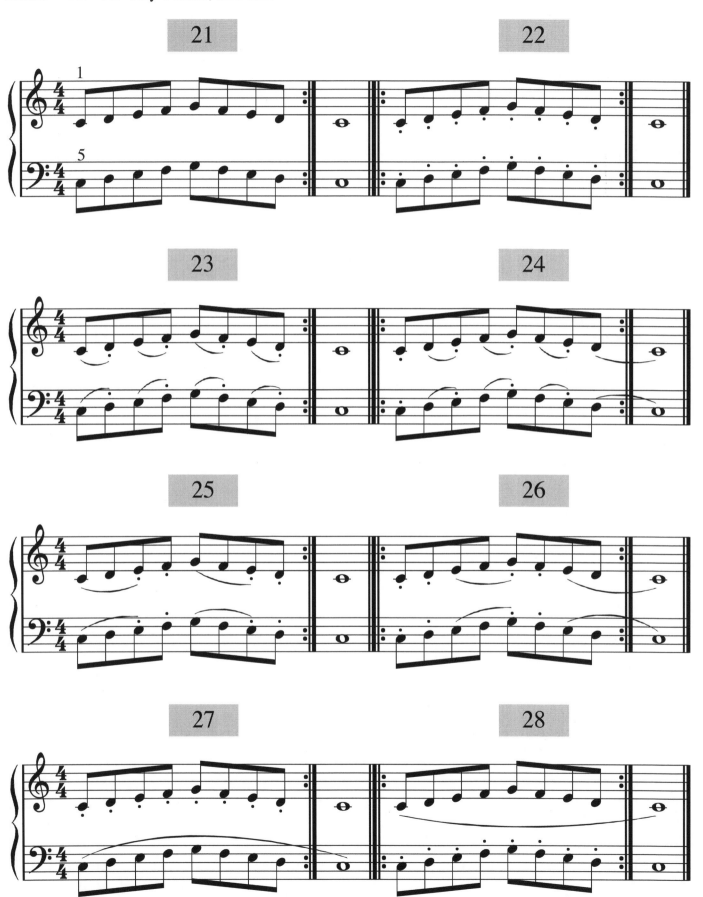

Finger Switching

M.M. = 76 - 92

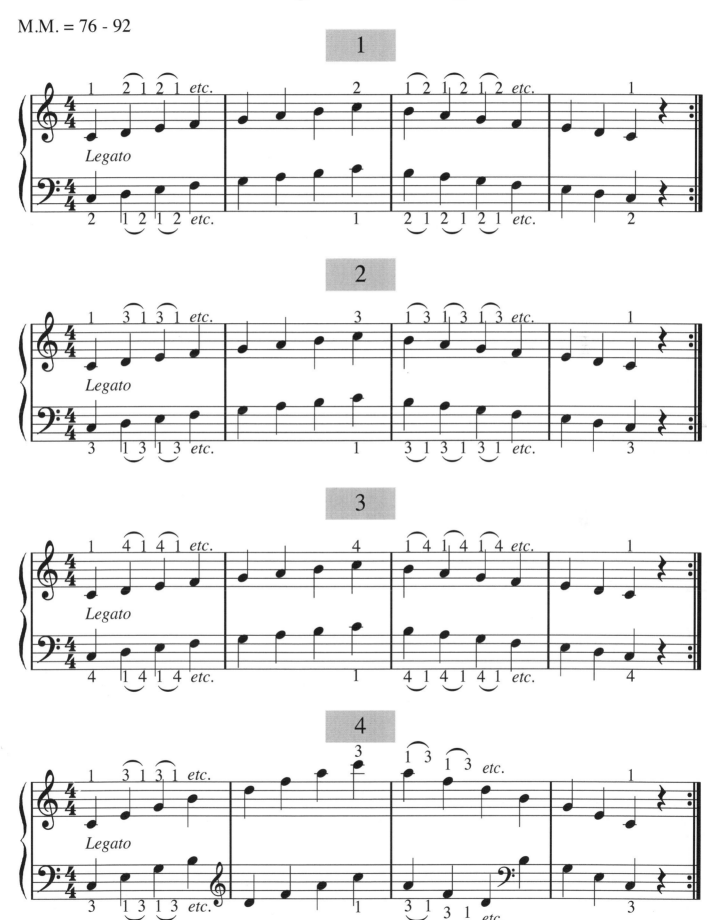

M.M. = 76 - 92

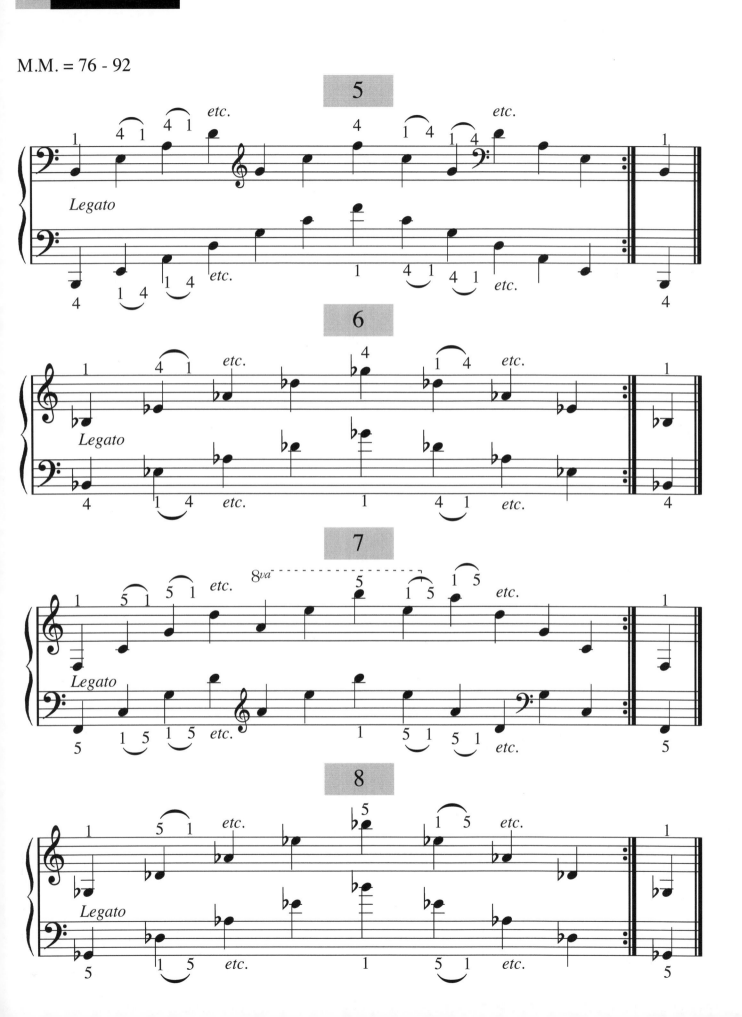

Hand Jumps

Keep the hand in a relaxed shape throughout, never widening the hand toward an octave reach. Use the forearm to measure the distance back and forth as the hand quickly moves across the keyboard.

M.M. = 92 - 108

M.M. = 92 - 108

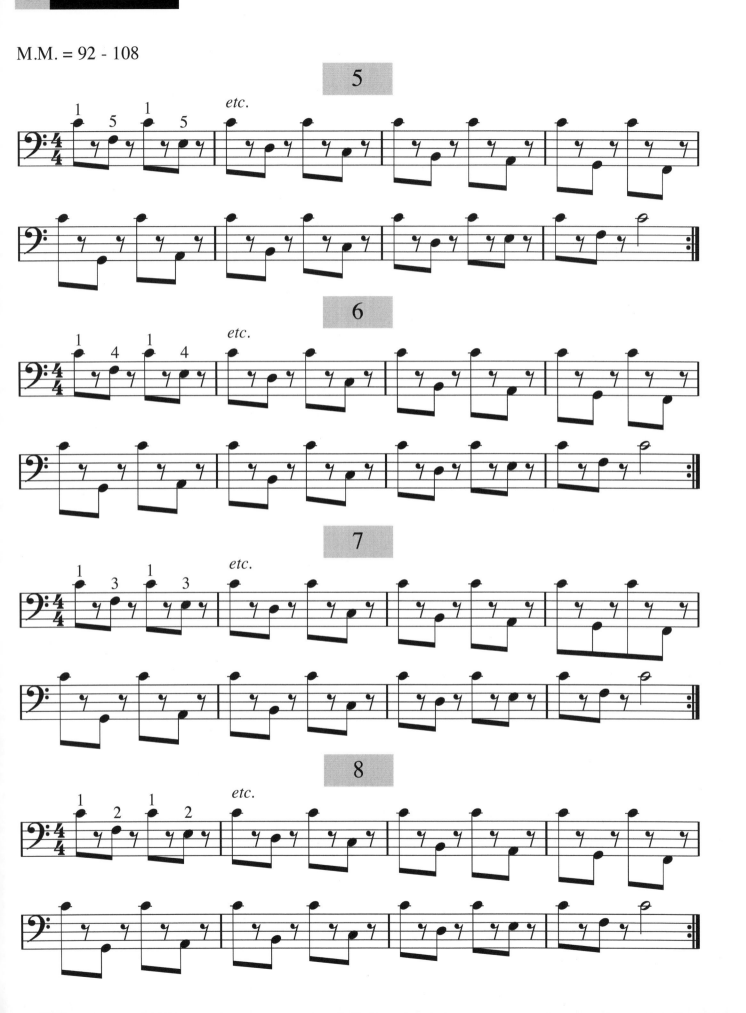

M.M. = 92 - 108

M.M. = 92 - 108

Wrist Rotation

Wrist rotation means to tilt the wrist back and forth between the thumb and pinky sides of the hand. This propels the fingers and should be maintained throughout each exercies. Limit the range to five or six keys for smaller hands, adjusting the pattern to maintain meter and accent placement.

Contrary Motion

M.M. = 132 - 160 Play 4 times, then end.

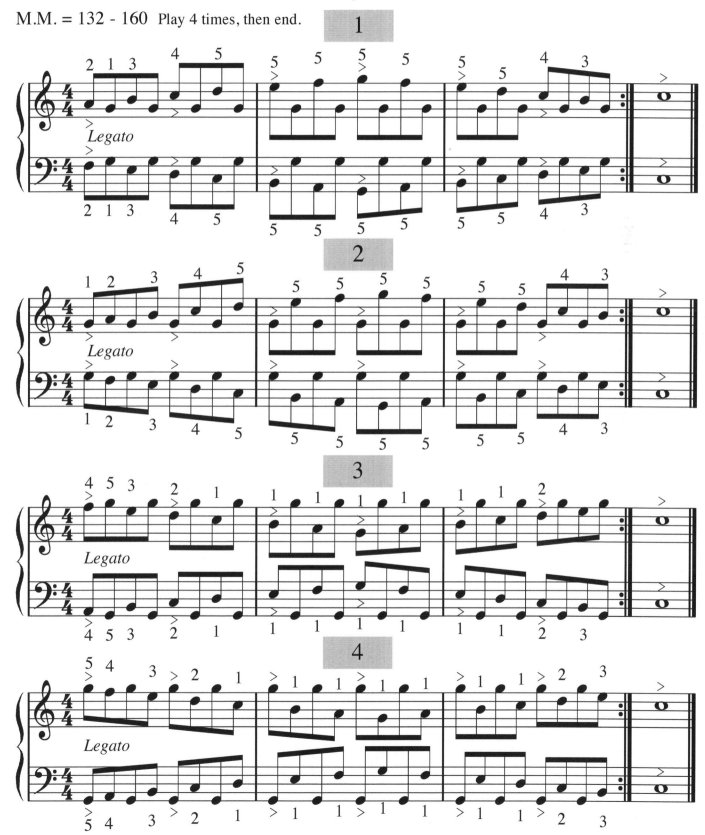

Parallel Motion

M.M. = 132 - 160 Play 4 times, then end.

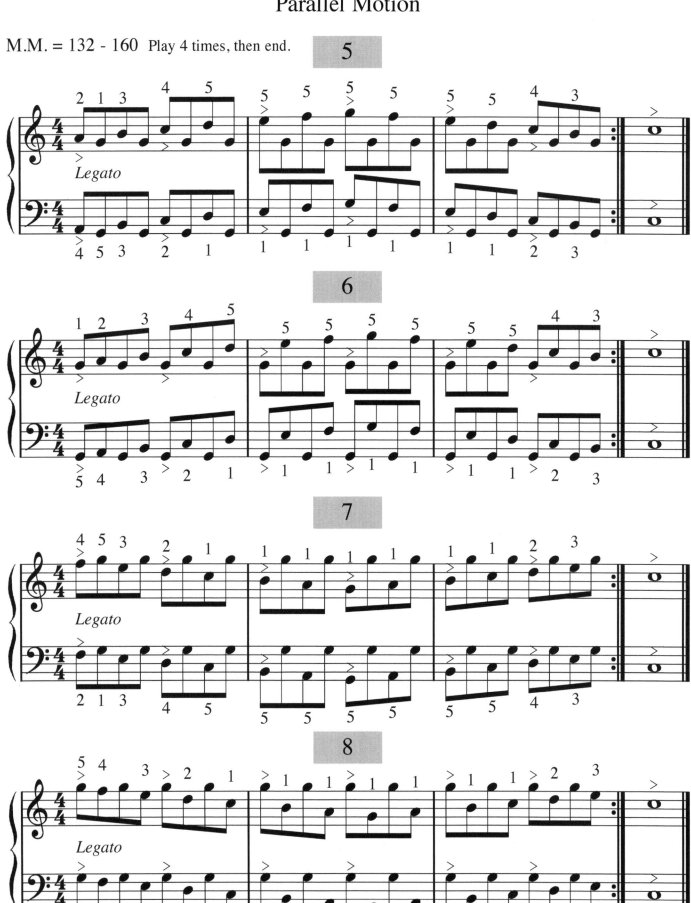

Trills

Practice trills using a combination of both rapid finger movement (close to the keys) and wrist rotation. The amount of rotation will vary, depending on individual finger pairings. Begin slowly.

M.M. = 66 - 76

M.M. = 76 - 88

3

M.M. = 76 - 88

Mozart's trill

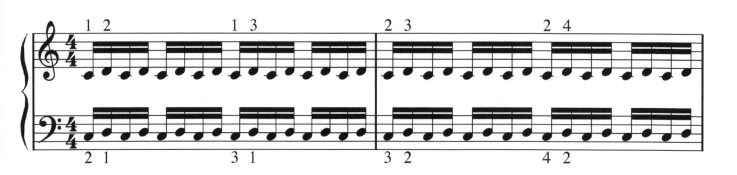

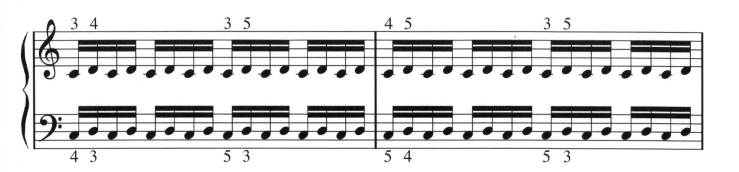

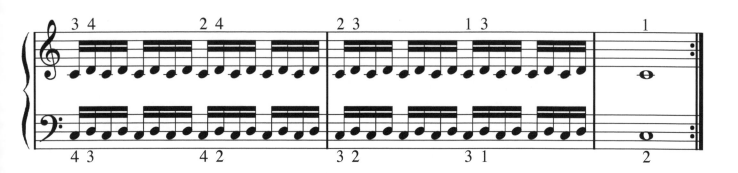

4

M.M. = 76 - 88

Thalberg's trill

Play 4 times, then end.

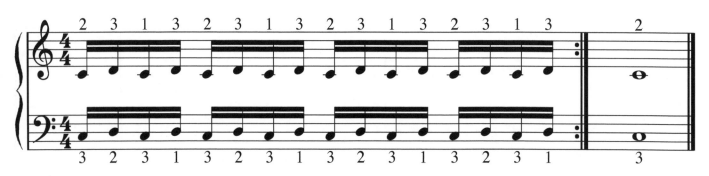

Tremolos

Like trills, tremolos are played using a combination of both rapid finger movement (close to the keys) and wrist rotation. Rotation amount will vary, depending on finger pairings. Begin slowly, gradually working up to the suggested tempo range.

M.M. = 76 - 88

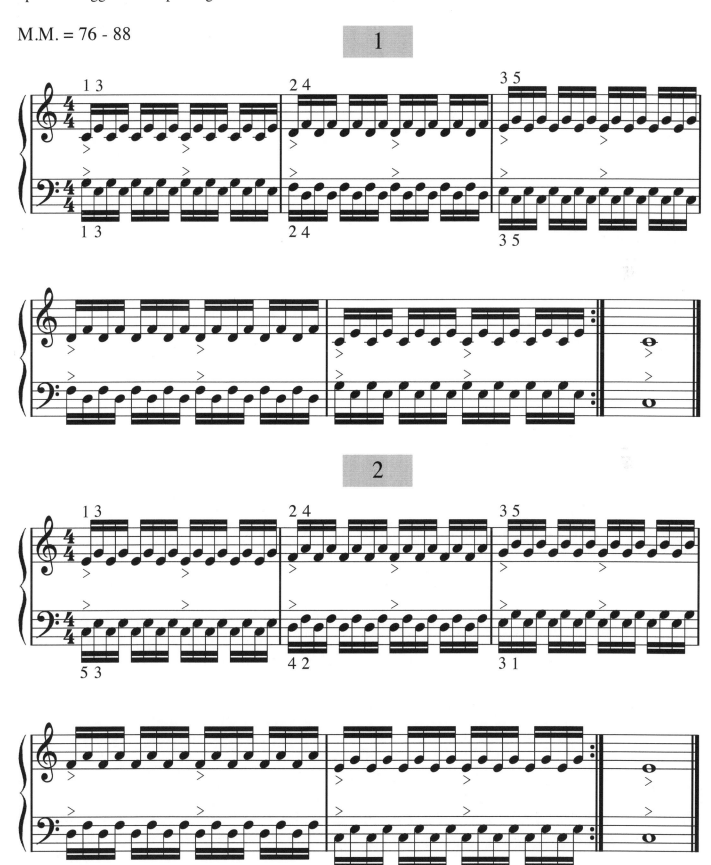

3

4

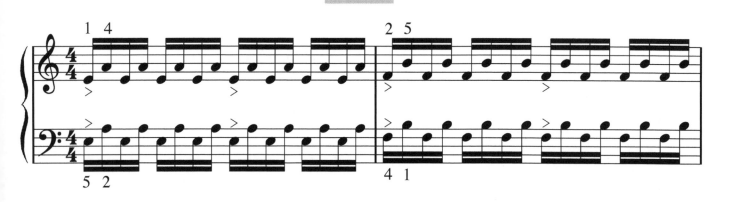

Wrist Strokes

The wrist remains loose and flexible during the up and down movement of each stroke, while the fingertips maintain a firm, slightly curved position. Keep the forearms relaxed to facilitate wrist movement and reduce fatigue. Finger 4 or 3 may be used in place of finger 5, especially with larger hands.

Wrist Stroke Exercise #1 focuses on rhythm as well as wrist technique. Inaccuracies typically occur when transitioning from one rhythm into another and, in particular, when going from a faster to slower rhythm. Isolate and practice inaccurate transitions until they are precise.

M.M. = 60 - 72

1

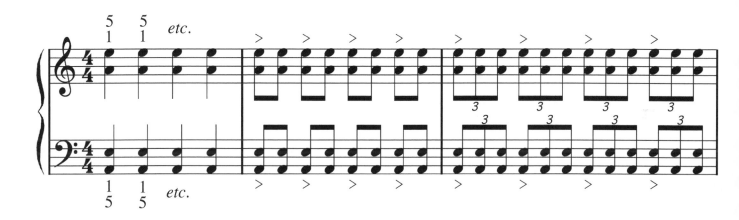

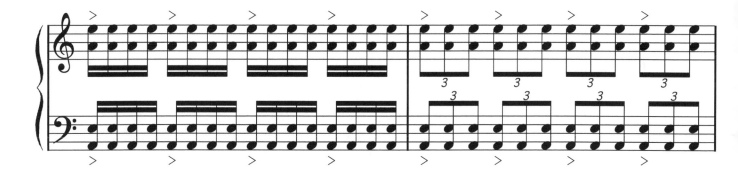

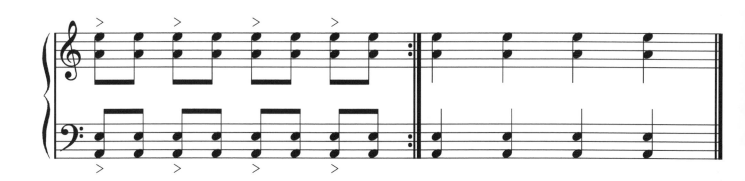

M.M. = 80 - 100   Play 4 times, then end.

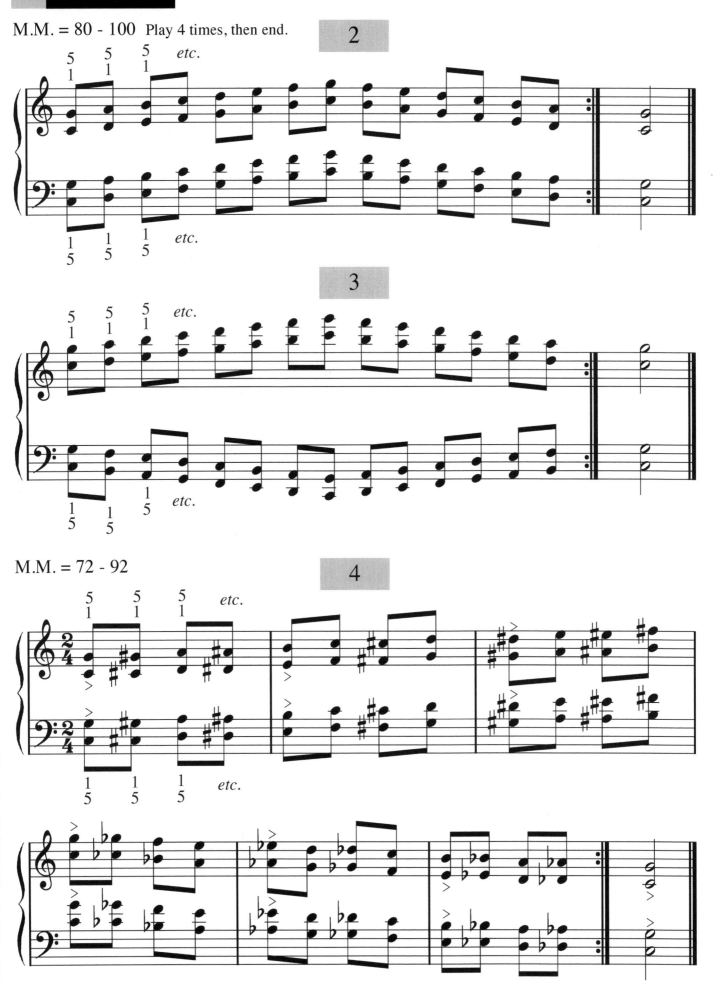

Repeated Notes
One Finger Per Key

M.M. = 104 - 120

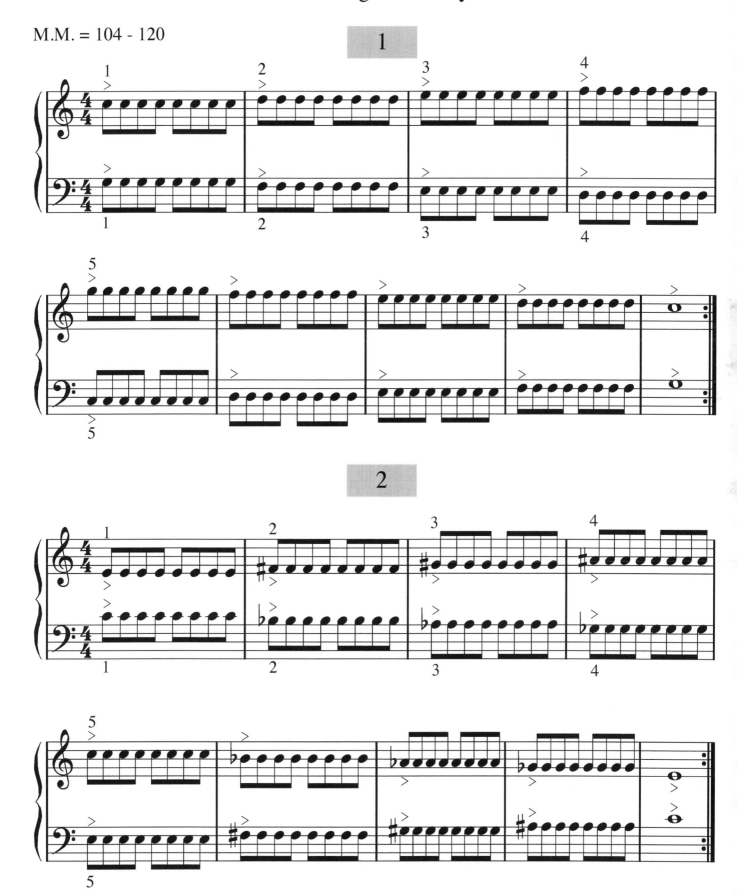

Two Fingers Per Key

M.M. = 108 - 132

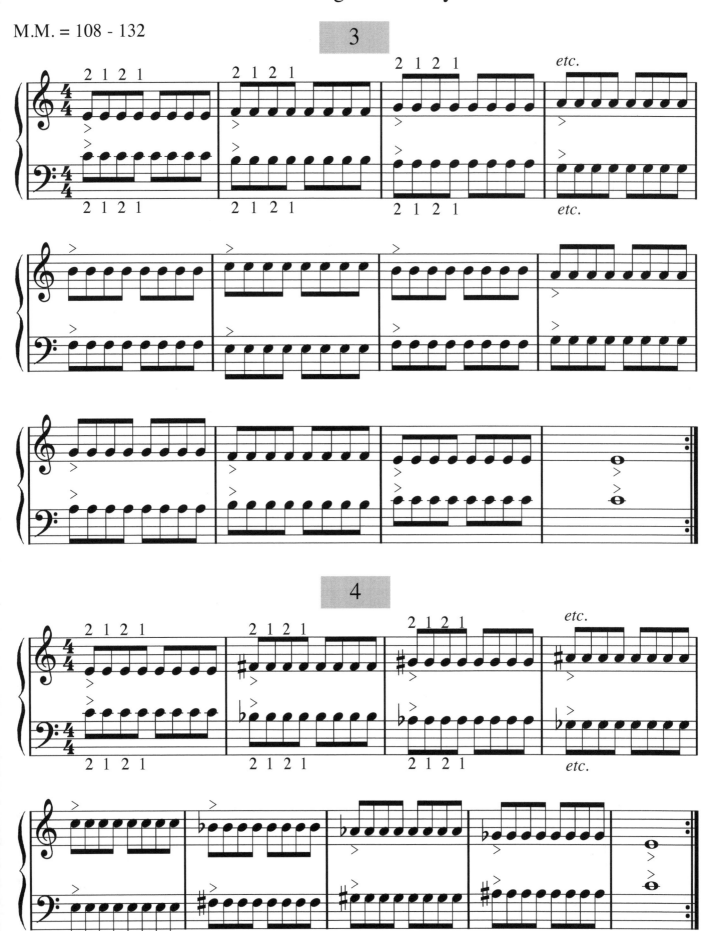

Three Fingers Per Key

M.M. = 88 - 108

Four Fingers Per Key

M.M. = 66 - 80

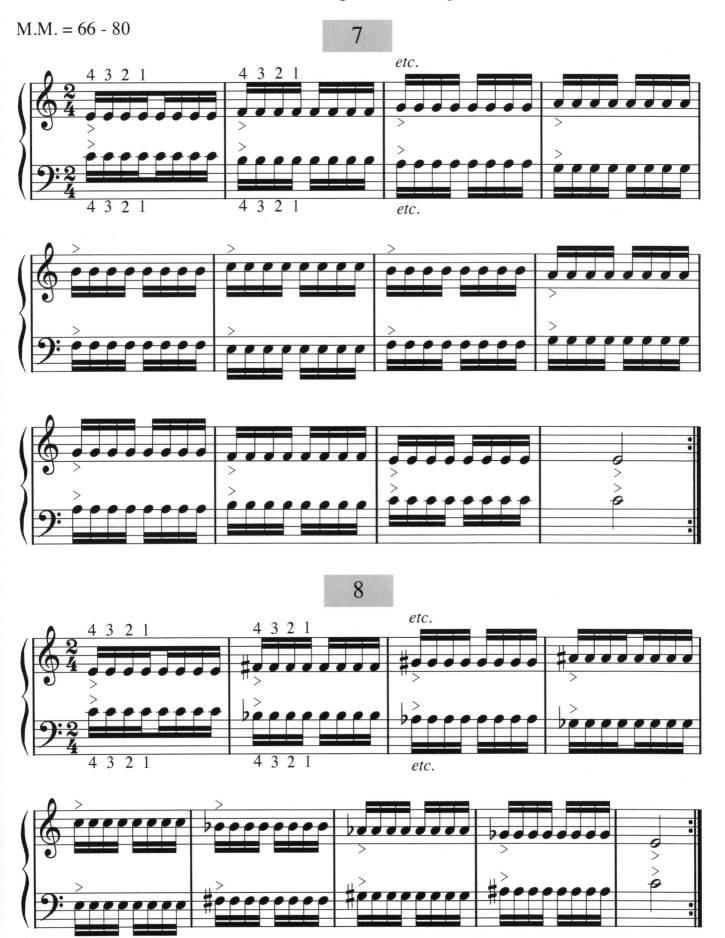

Finger Independence

M.M. = 72 - 92   Play 8 times, then end.

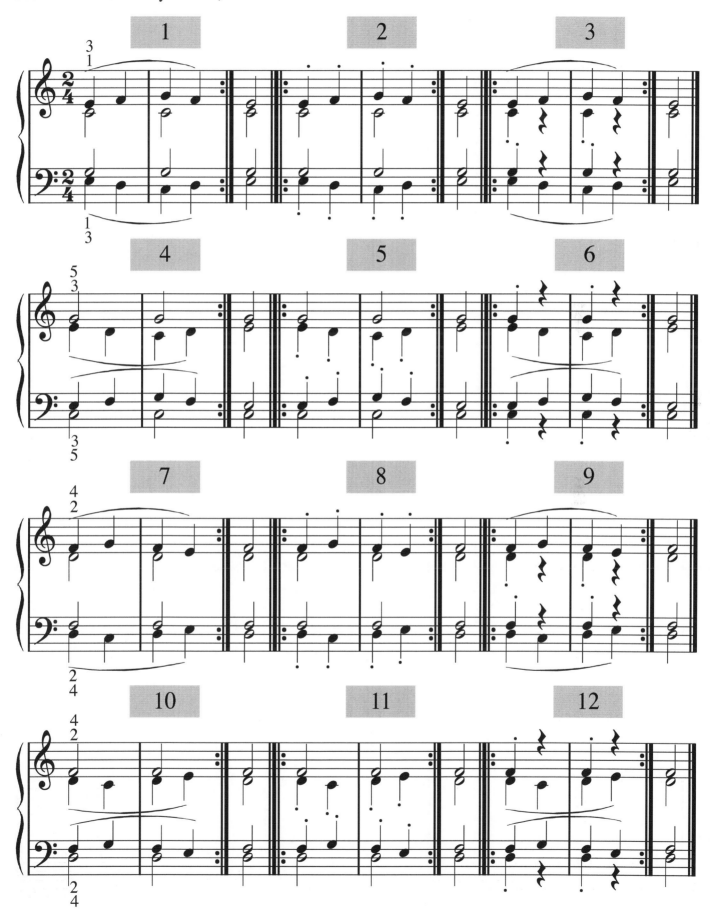

M.M. = 108 - 132 Play 8 times, then end. Opening whole notes are held down throughout each exercise.

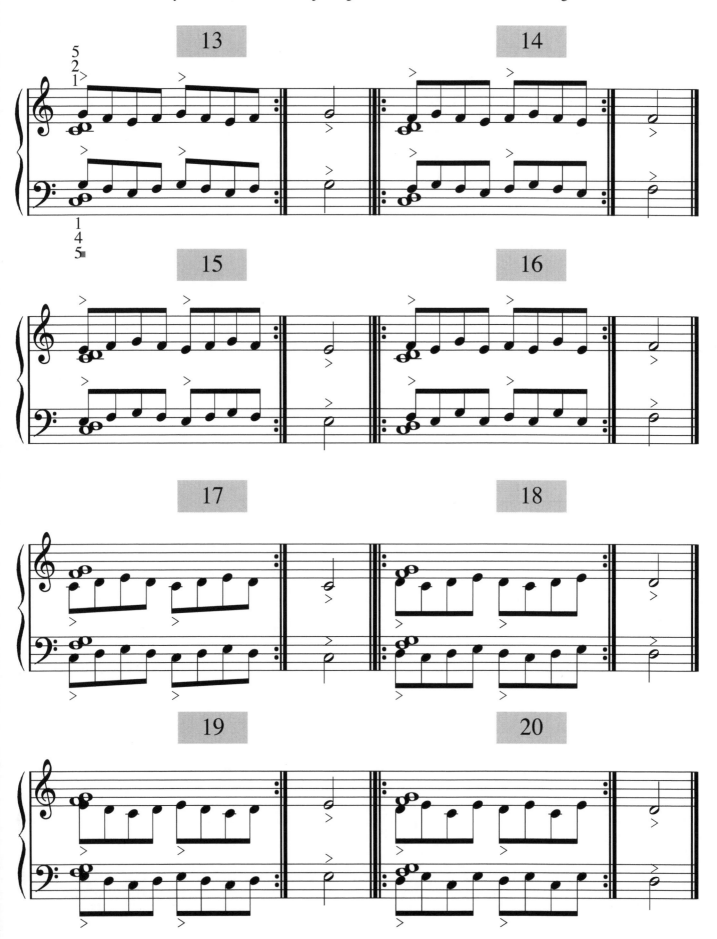

M.M. = 80 - 100

21

22

M.M. = 60 - 80

23

Hold all keys except the one being played.

Thirds

M.M. = 92 - 112 Play 8 times, then end.

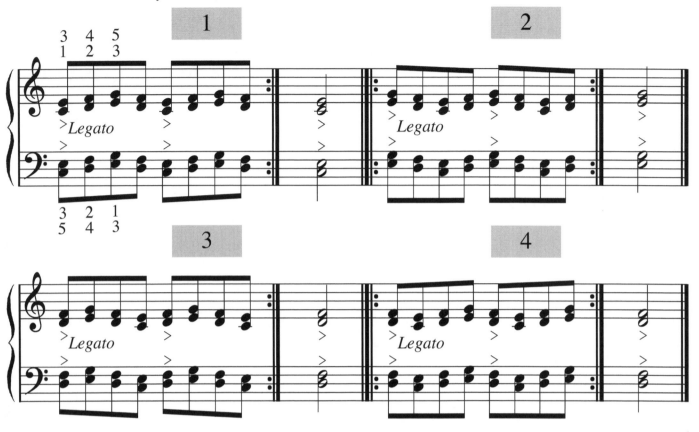

M.M. = 54 - 66 Play 8 times, then end.

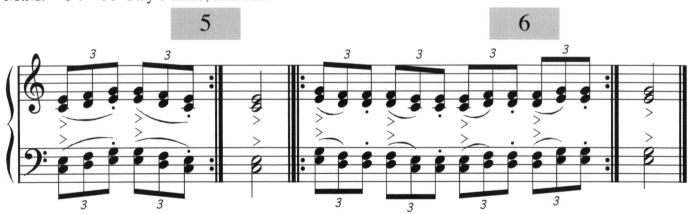

M.M. = 72 - 92 Play 8 times, then end.

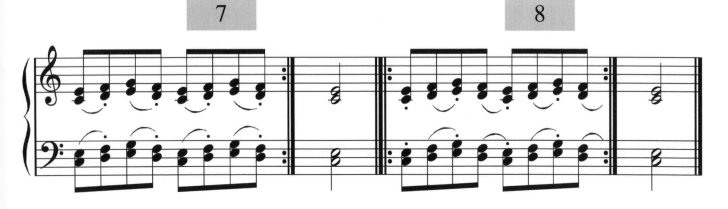

Hand Over Hand - One Hand Static

In the static hand (playing middle C), finger 3 is near the front of its key, allowing the crossing hand to move more easily in a back-and-forth arc over the static hand. In the crossing hand, the wrist tilts downward from an elevated position with finger 3 slightly extended. Maintain this posture throughout.

M.M. = 112 - 126

Wrist Turning

M.M. = 66 - 80 Play 8 times, then end. Opening half notes are held down throughout each exercise.

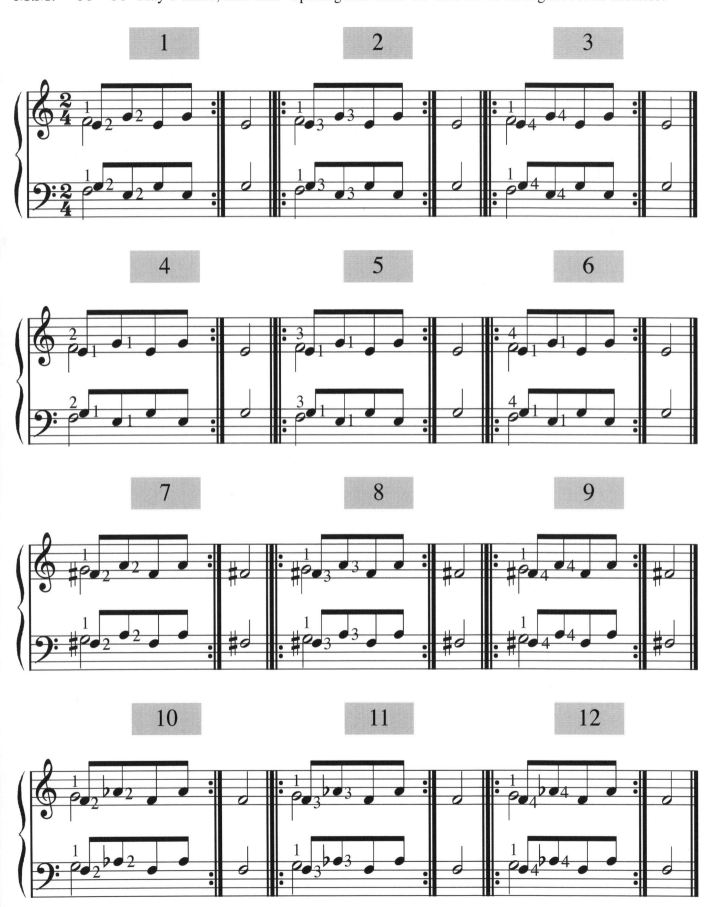

Essential Piano and Keyboard Technique

Section 2 Checksheet

Scales

✓	PROJECTS
☐	C Major Scale and Preparations
☐	G Major Scale and Preparations
☐	D Major Scale and Preparations
☐	A Major Scale and Preparations
☐	E Major Scale and Preparations
☐	B Major Scale and Preparations
☐	F♯ Major Scale and Preparations
☐	C♯ Major Scale and Preparations
☐	C♭, G♭ and D♭ Major Scales
☐	A♭ Major Scale and Preparations
☐	E♭ Major Scale and Preparations
☐	B♭ Major Scale and Preparations
☐	F Major Scale and Preparations
☐	Natural Minor Scales
☐	Harmonic Minor Scales
☐	Melodic Minor Scales
☐	Chromatic Scale - Parallel & Contrary Motion
☐	Whole Tone Scales
☐	Modes of the C Major Scale
☐	Scale Variation #1
☐	Scale Variations #2 - 6
☐	Scale Variation #7
☐	Scale Variations #8 - 11

(over)

✓   PROJECTS

- [ ] 2:3 Polyrhythm Preparation #1 - 2
- [ ] 2:3 Polyrhythm - One Octave
- [ ] 2:3 Polyrhythm - Three Octaves
- [ ] Major Scales in Thirds or Tenths
- [ ] Major Scales in Sixths
- [ ] Chromatic Scale in Octaves
- [ ] Major Scales in Octaves
- [ ] Harmonic Minor Scales in Octaves
- [ ] Major Scales in Broken Octaves
- [ ] C Major Scale in Double Thirds - Staccato
- [ ] C Major Scale in Double Thirds - Legato
- [ ] C Major Scale in Double Sixths - Staccato
- [ ] C Major Scale - Hand Over Hand

C Major Scale Preparations

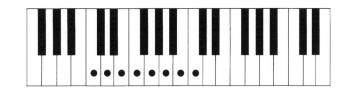

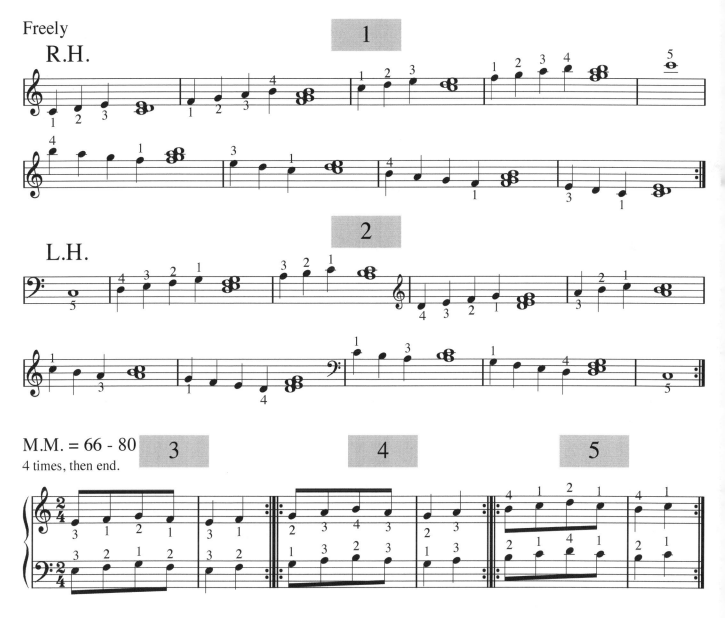

C Major Scale

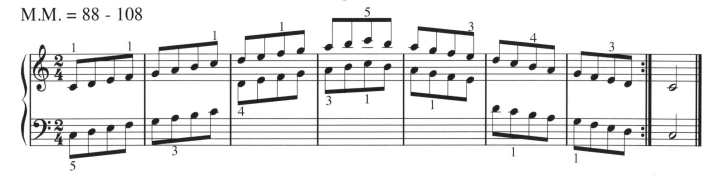

G Major Scale Preparations

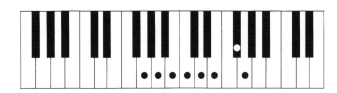

Freely

1

R.H.

2

L.H.

M.M. = 66 - 80
4 times, then end.

3   **4**   **5**

G Major Scale

M.M. = 88 - 108

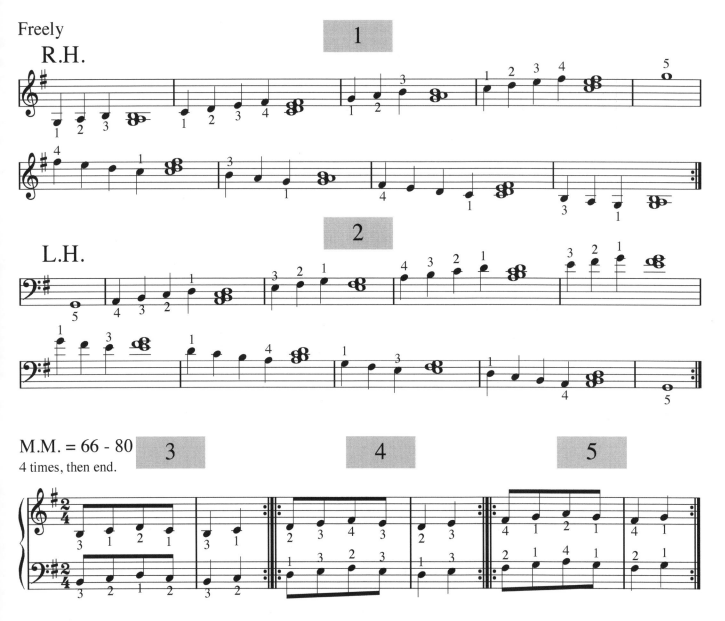
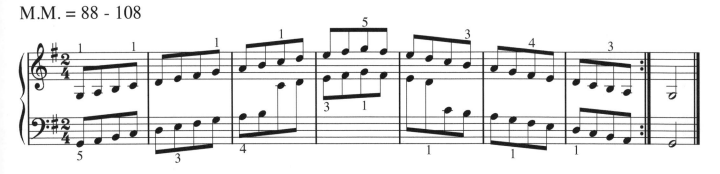

D Major Scale Preparations

D Major Scale

A Major Scale Preparations

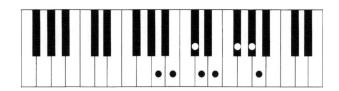

Freely

R.H.

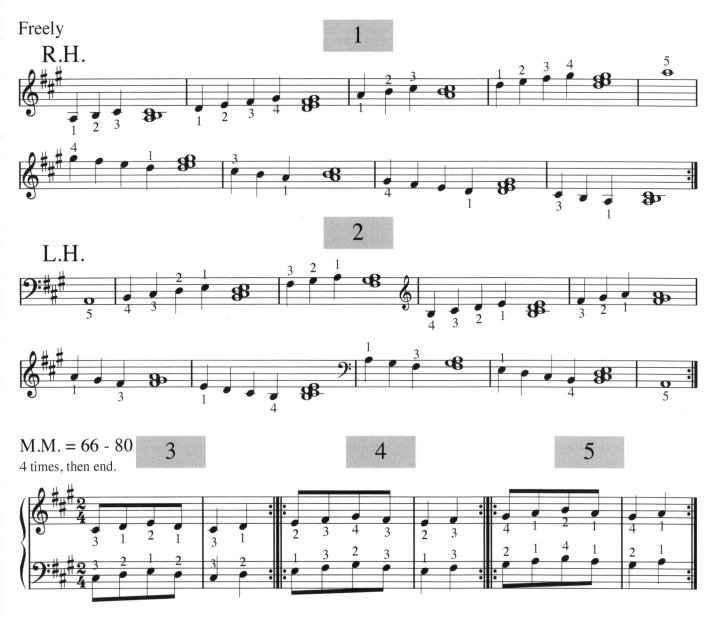

L.H.

M.M. = 66 - 80
4 times, then end.

A Major Scale

M.M. = 88 - 108

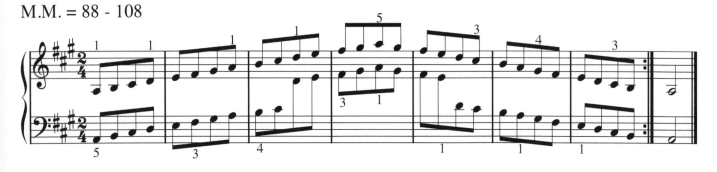

E Major Scale Preparations

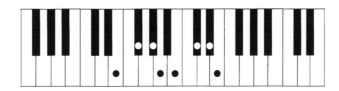

Freely

E Major Scale

M.M. = 88 - 108

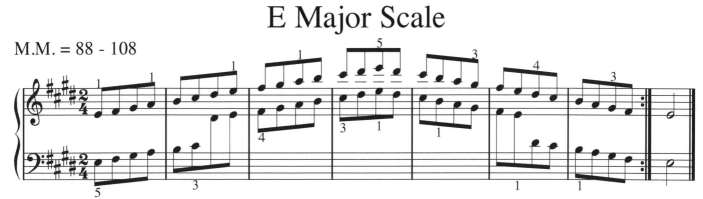

B Major Scale Preparations

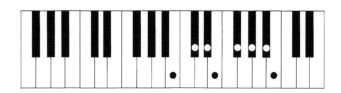

Freely

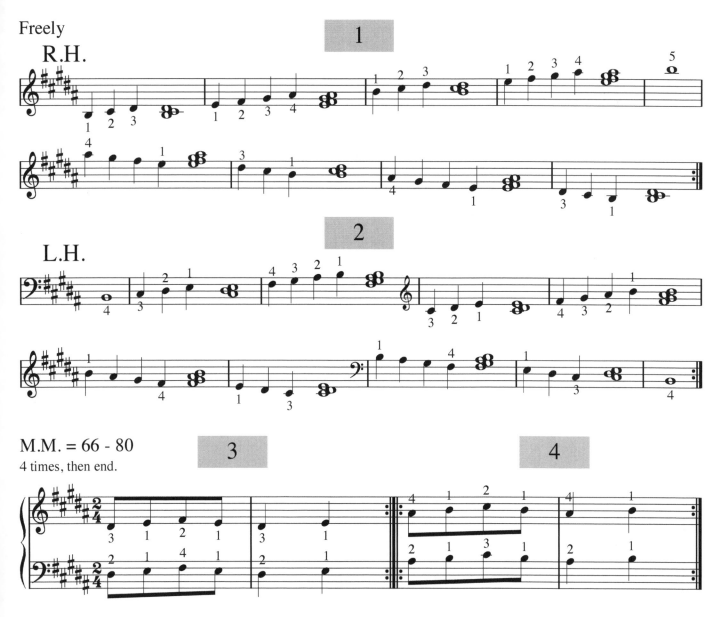

1

2

M.M. = 66 - 80
4 times, then end.

3   4

B Major Scale

M.M. = 88 - 108

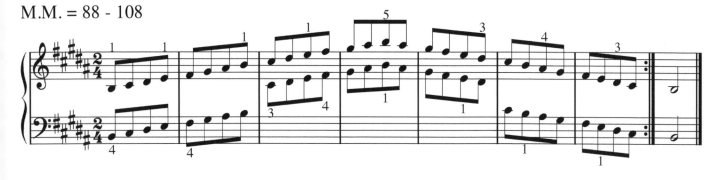

F# Major Scale Preparations

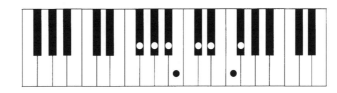

Freely

1

R.H.

2

L.H.

M.M. = 66 - 80
4 times, then end.

3   **4**

F# Major Scale

M.M. = 88 - 108

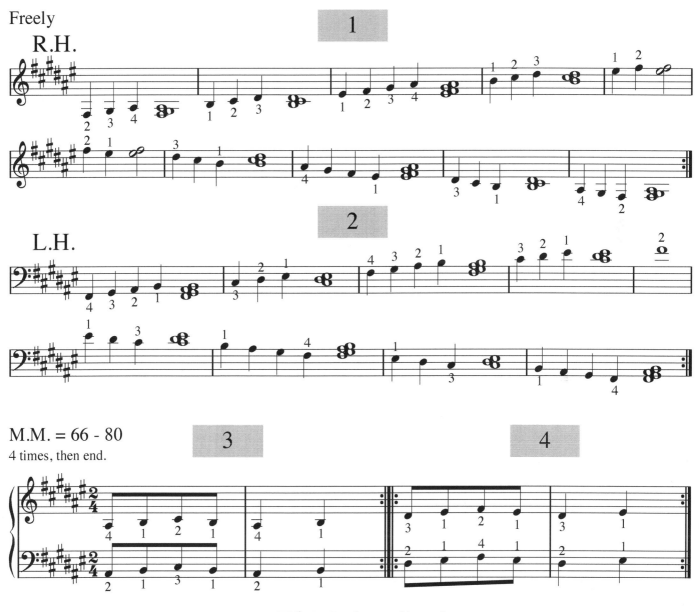

C♯ Major Scale Preparations

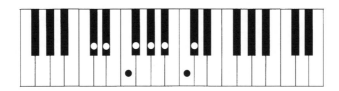

Freely

1

R.H.

2

L.H.

M.M. = 66 - 80
4 times, then end.

3   **4**

C♯ Major Scale

M.M. = 88 - 108

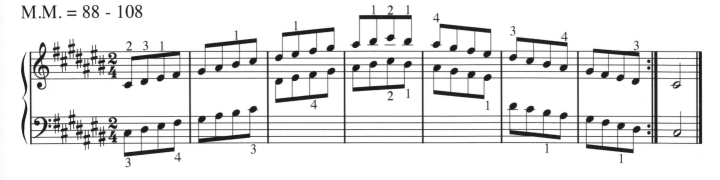

Note: The following three scales need no preparations since they are played exactly the same as their respective enharmonic equivalents.

C♭ Major Scale (Enharmonic of B Major)

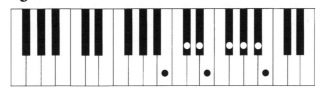

M.M. = 88 - 108

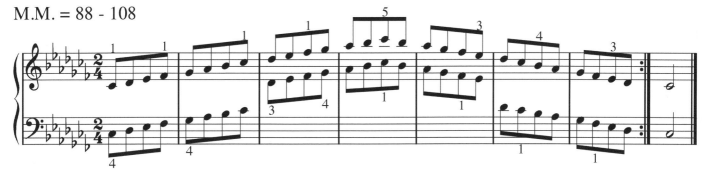

G♭ Major Scale (Enharmonic of F♯ Major)

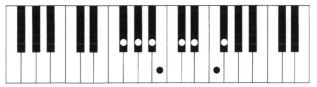

M.M. = 88 - 108

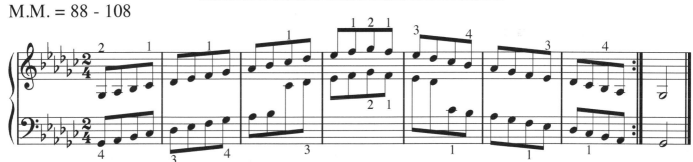

D♭ Major Scale (Enharmonic of C♯ Major)

M.M. = 88 - 108

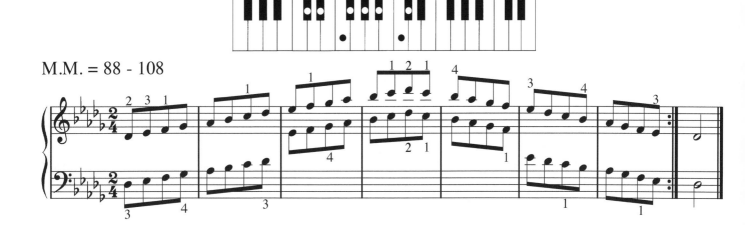

A♭ Major Scale Preparations

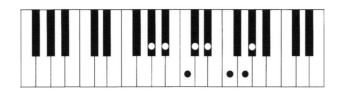

Freely

R.H.

1

L.H.

2

M.M. = 66 - 80

4 times, then end.

3   **4**   **5**

A♭ Major Scale

M.M. = 88 - 108

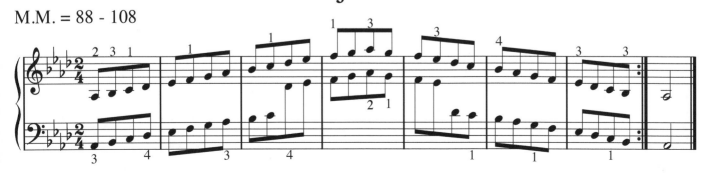

E♭ Major Scale Preparations

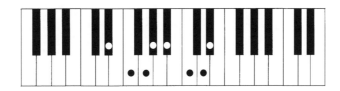

Freely

M.M. = 66 - 80
4 times, then end.

E♭ Major Scale

M.M. = 88 - 108

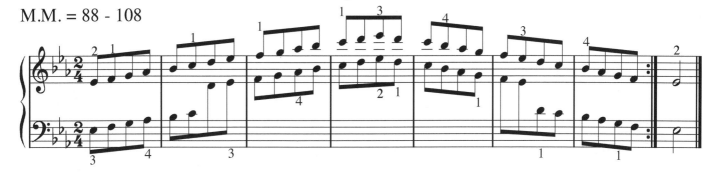

B♭ Major Scale Preparations

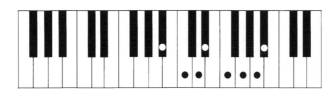

Freely

1

R.H.

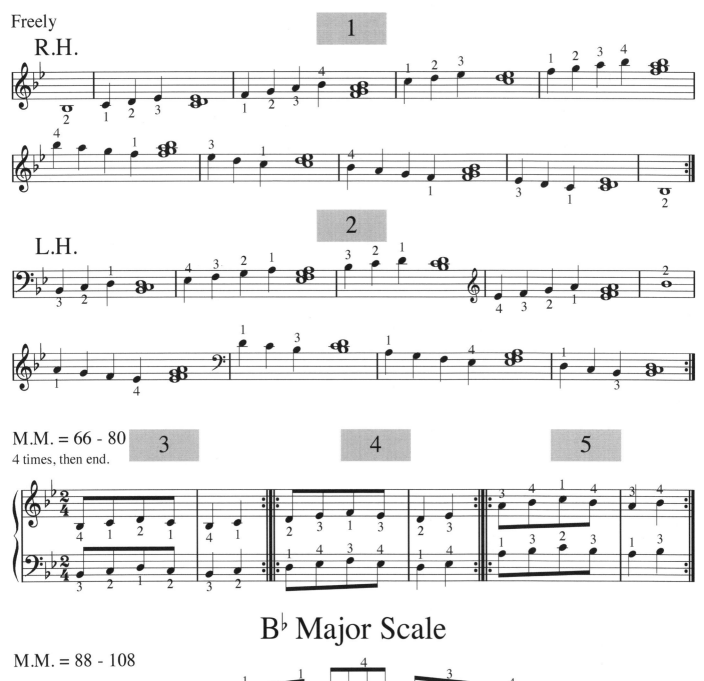

L.H.

2

M.M. = 66 - 80

4 times, then end.

3　　　　**4**　　　　**5**

B♭ Major Scale

M.M. = 88 - 108

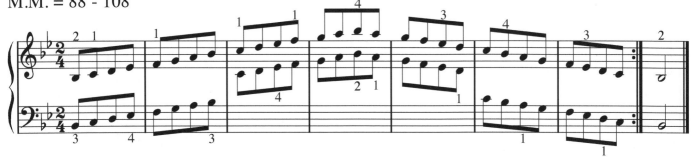

F Major Scale Preparations

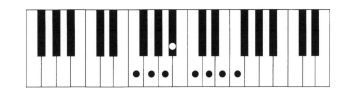

Freely

R.H.

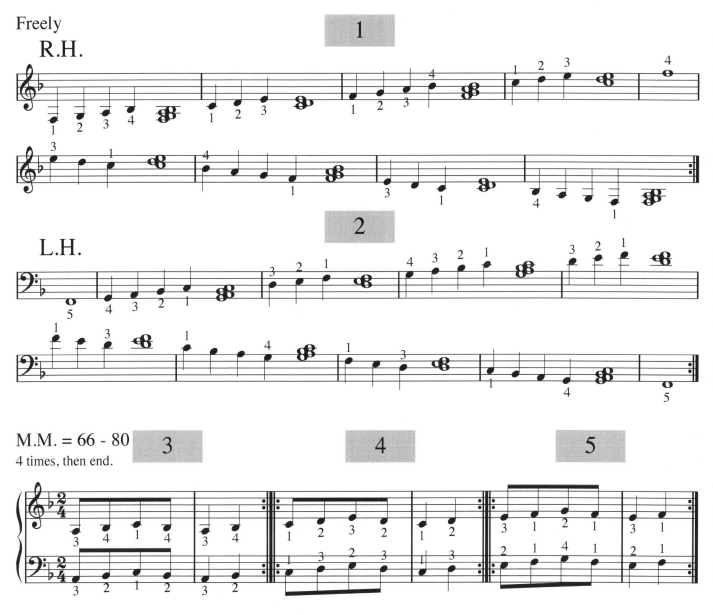

L.H.

M.M. = 66 - 80

4 times, then end.

F Major Scale

M.M. = 88 - 108

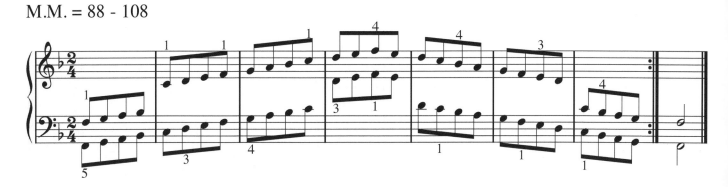

A Natural Minor Scale

Relative Minor of
C Major

M.M. = 88 - 108

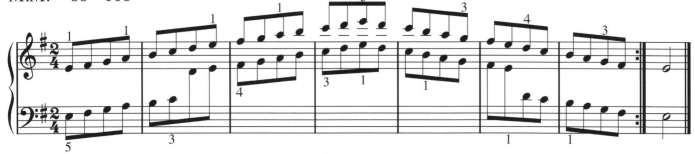

E Natural Minor Scale

Relative Minor of
G Major

M.M. = 88 - 108

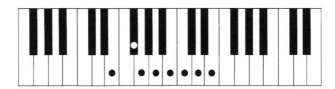

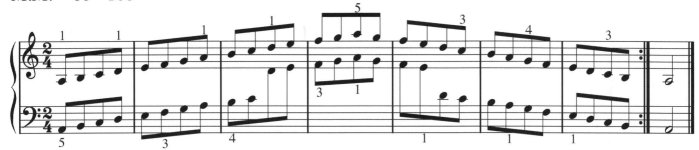

B Natural Minor Scale

Relative Minor of
D Major

M.M. = 88 - 108

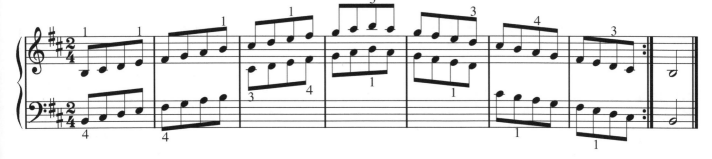

F♯ Natural Minor Scale

Relative Minor of
A Major

M.M. = 88 - 108

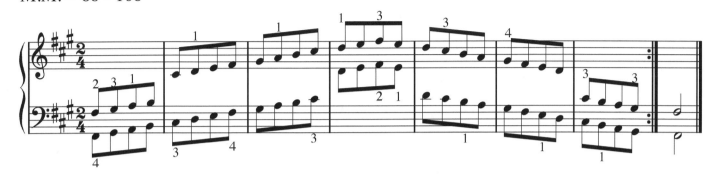

C♯ Natural Minor Scale

Relative Minor of
E Major

M.M. = 88 - 108

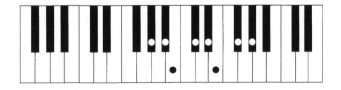

G♯ Natural Minor Scale (Enharmonic of A♭ Natural Minor)

Relative Minor of
B Major

M.M. = 88 - 108

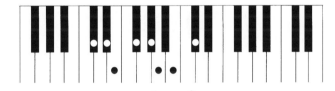

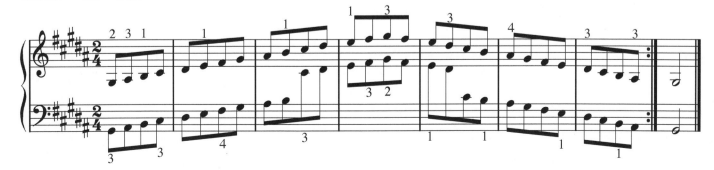

D♯ Natural Minor Scale (Enharmonic of E♭ Natural Minor)

Relative Minor of
F♯ Major

M.M. = 88 - 108

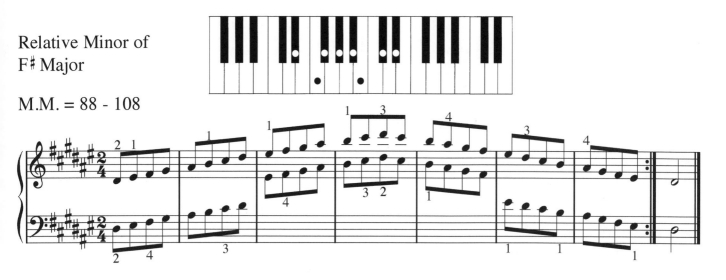

A♯ Natural Minor Scale (Enharmonic of B♭ Natural Minor)

Relative Minor of
C♯ Major

M.M. = 88 - 108

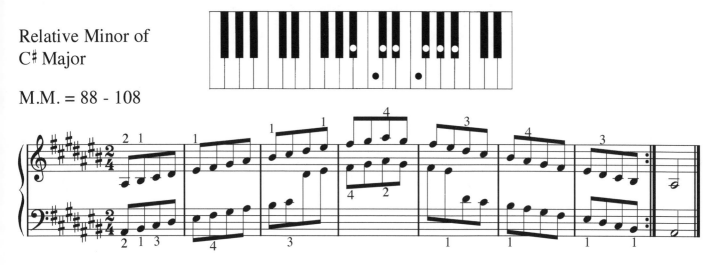

A♭ Natural Minor Scale (Enharmonic of G♯ Natural Minor)

Relative Minor of
C♭ Major

M.M. = 88 - 108

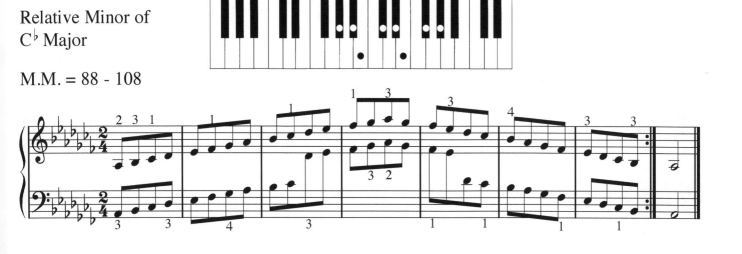

E♭ Natural Minor Scale (Enharmonic of D♯ Natural Minor)

Relative Minor of
G♭ Major

M.M. = 88 - 108

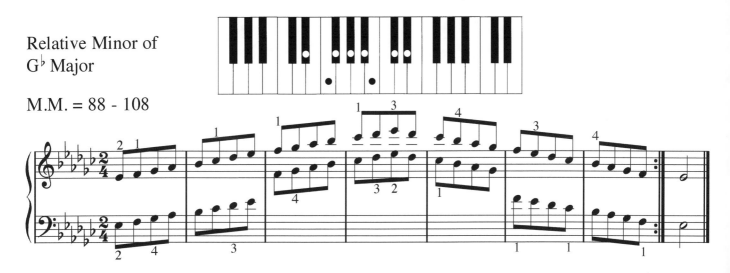

B♭ Natural Minor Scale (Enharmonic of A♯ Natural Minor)

Relative Minor of
D♭ Major

M.M. = 88 - 108

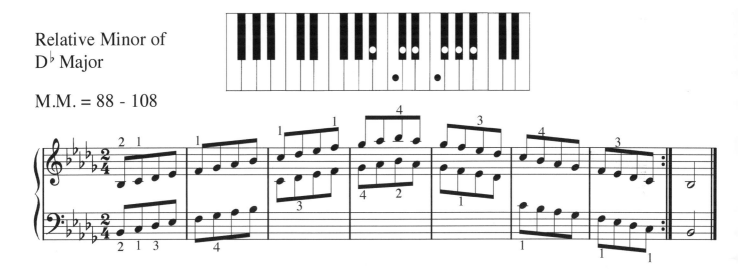

F Natural Minor Scale

Relative Minor of
A♭ Major

M.M. = 88 - 108

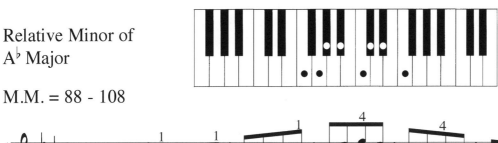

C Natural Minor Scale

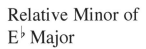

Relative Minor of
E♭ Major

M.M. = 88 - 108

G Natural Minor Scale

Relative Minor of
B♭ Major

M.M. = 88 - 108

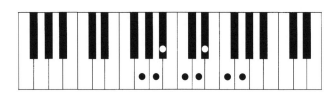

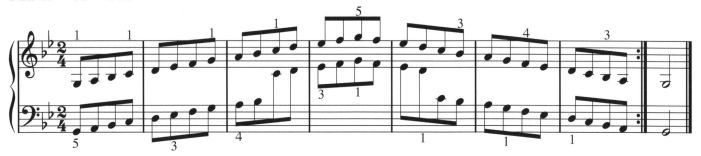

D Natural Minor Scale

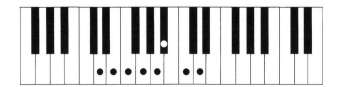

Relative Minor of
F Major

M.M. = 88 - 108

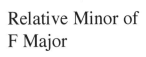

A Harmonic Minor Scale

Relative Minor of
C Major

M.M. = 88 - 108

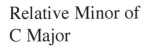

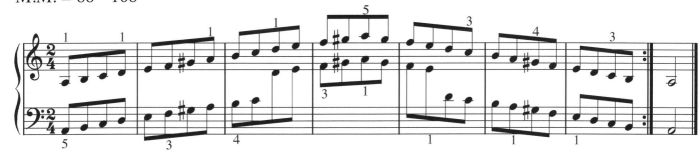

E Harmonic Minor Scale

Relative Minor of
G Major

M.M. = 88 - 108

B Harmonic Minor Scale

Relative Minor of
D Major

M.M. = 88 - 108

F# Harmonic Minor Scale

Relative Minor of
A Major

M.M. = 88 - 108

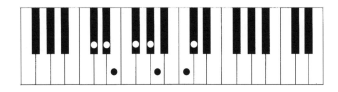

C# Harmonic Minor Scale

Relative Minor of
E Major

M.M. = 88 - 108

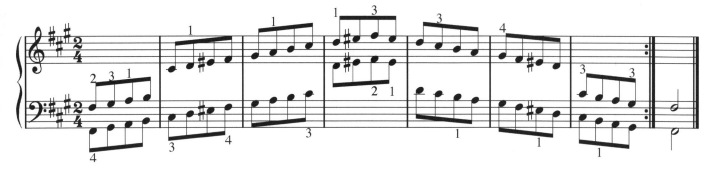

G# Harmonic Minor Scale (Enharmonic of A♭ Harmonic Minor)

Relative Minor of
B Major

M.M. = 88 - 108

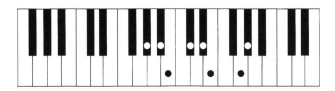

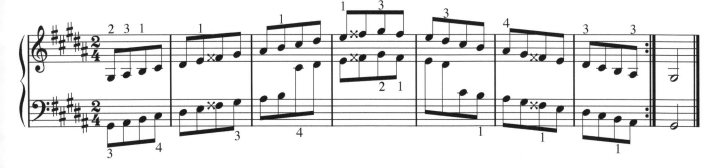

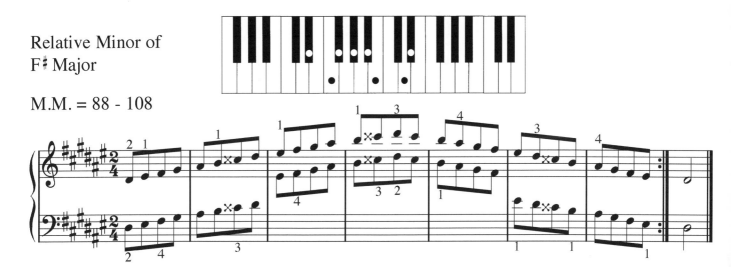

D♯ Harmonic Minor Scale (Enharmonic of E♭ Harmonic Minor)

Relative Minor of
F♯ Major

M.M. = 88 - 108

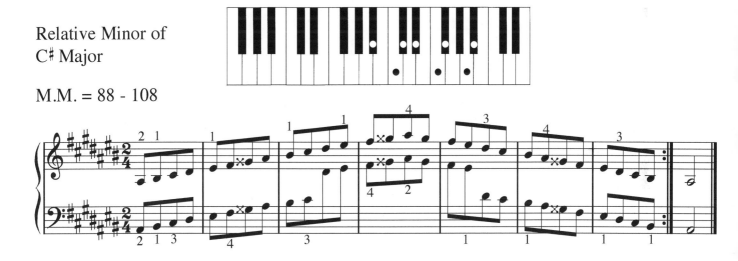

A♯ Harmonic Minor Scale (Enharmonic of B♭ Harmonic Minor)

Relative Minor of
C♯ Major

M.M. = 88 - 108

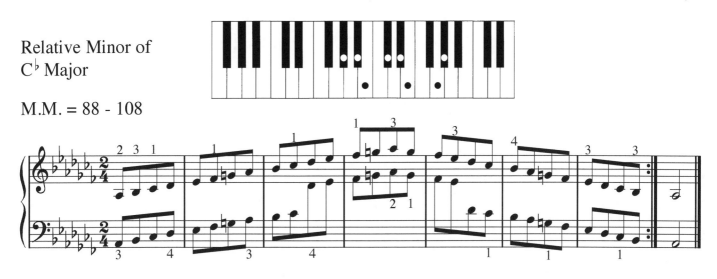

A♭ Harmonic Minor Scale (Enharmonic of G♯ Harmonic Minor)

Relative Minor of
C♭ Major

M.M. = 88 - 108

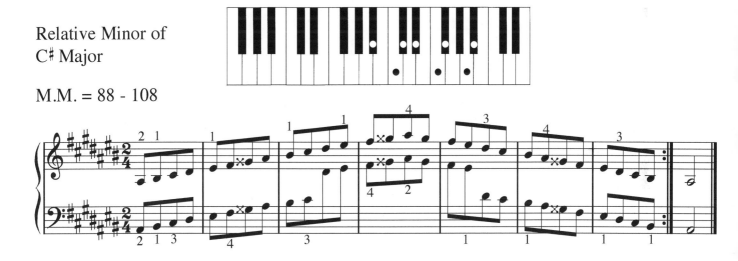

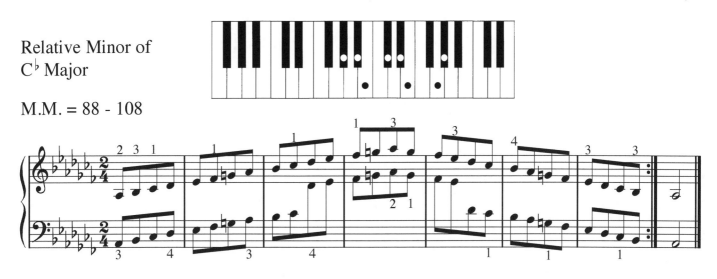

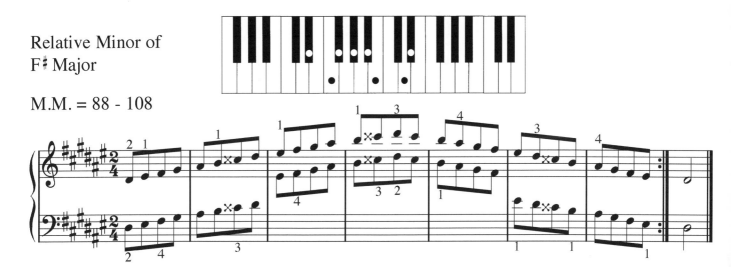

E♭ Harmonic Minor Scale (Enharmonic of D♯ Harmonic Minor)

Relative Minor of
G♭ Major

M.M. = 88 - 108

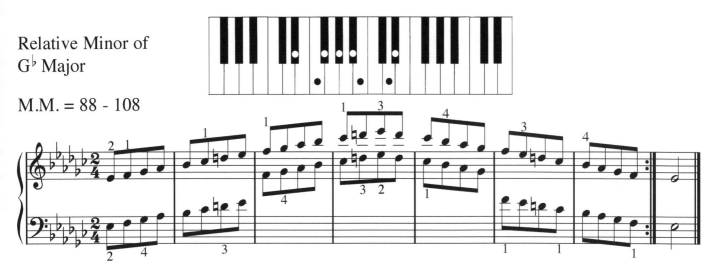

B♭ Harmonic Minor Scale (Enharmonic of A♯ Harmonic Minor)

Relative Minor of
D♭ Major

M.M. = 88 - 108

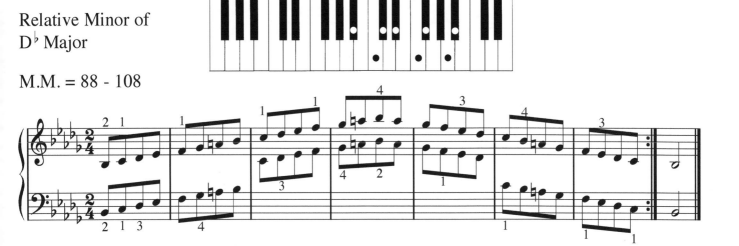

F Harmonic Minor Scale

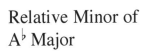

Relative Minor of
A♭ Major

M.M. = 88 - 108

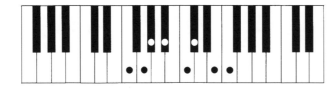

C Harmonic Minor Scale

Relative Minor of
E♭ Major

M.M. = 88 - 108

G Harmonic Minor Scale

Relative Minor of
B♭ Major

M.M. = 88 - 108

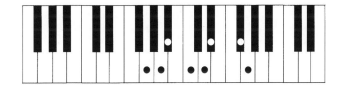

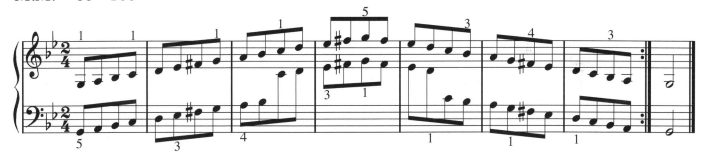

D Harmonic Minor Scale

Relative Minor of
F Major

M.M. = 88 - 108

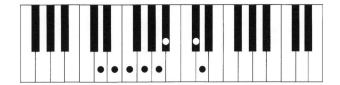

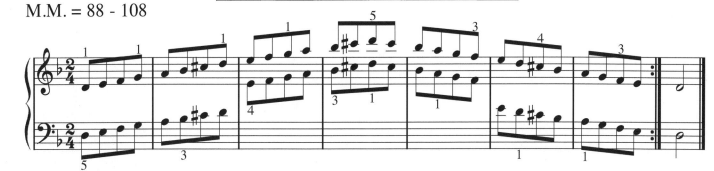

A Melodic Minor Scale

Relative Minor of
C Major

M.M. = 88 - 108

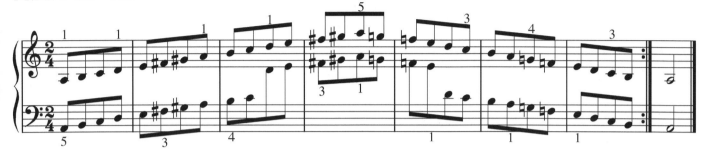

→ Ascending form shown.

Descending form is
A Natural Minor.

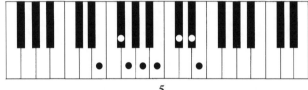

E Melodic Minor Scale

Relative Minor of
G Major

M.M. = 88 - 108

→ Ascending form shown.

Descending form is
E Natural Minor.

B Melodic Minor Scale

Relative Minor of
D Major

M.M. = 88 - 108

→ Ascending form shown.

Descending form is
B Natural Minor.

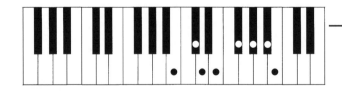

F# Melodic Minor Scale

Relative Minor of
A Major

M.M. = 88 - 108

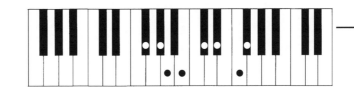

Ascending form only.

Descending form is
F# Natural Minor.

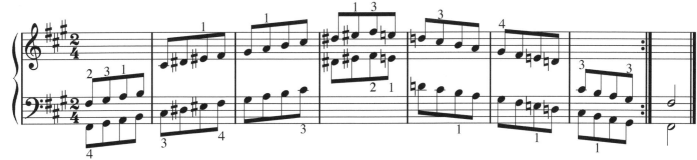

C# Melodic Minor Scale

Relative Minor of
E Major

M.M. = 88 - 108

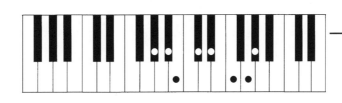

Ascending form only.

Descending form is
C# Natural Minor.

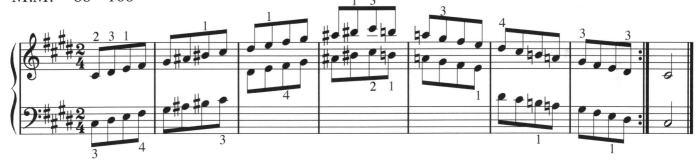

G# Melodic Minor Scale (Enharmonic of A♭ Melodic Minor)

Relative Minor of
B Major

M.M. = 88 - 108

Ascending form only.

Descending form is
G# Natural Minor.

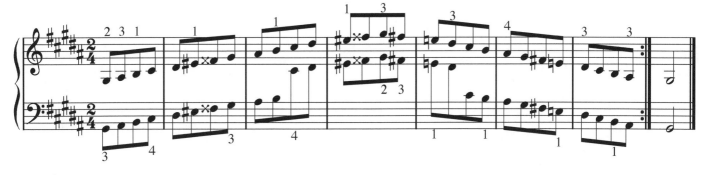

D♯ Melodic Minor Scale (Enharmonic of E♭ Melodic Minor)

Relative Minor of
F♯ Major

M.M. = 88 - 108

→ Ascending form only.

Descending form is
D♯ Natural Minor.

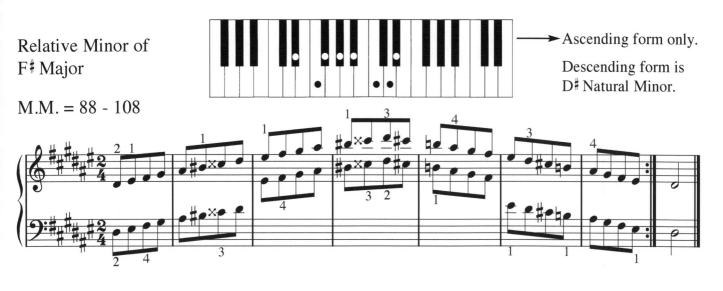

A♯ Melodic Minor Scale (Enharmonic of B♭ Melodic Minor)

Relative Minor of
C♯ Major

M.M. = 88 - 108

→ Ascending form only.

Descending form is
A♯ Natural Minor.

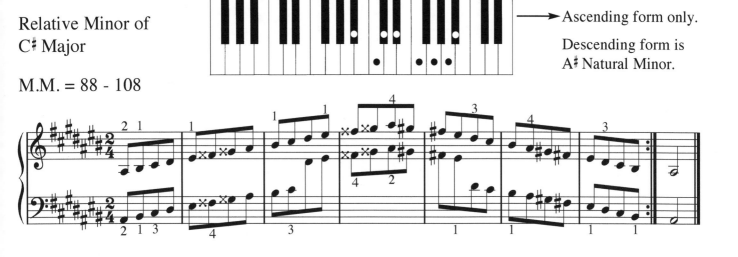

A♭ Melodic Minor Scale (Enharmonic of G♯ Melodic Minor)

Relative Minor of
C♭ Major

M.M. = 88 - 108

→ Ascending form only.

Descending form is
A♭ Natural Minor.

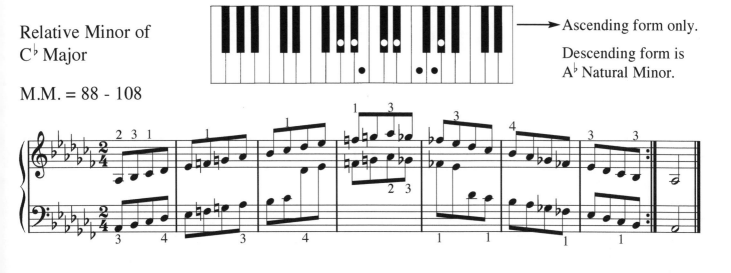

E♭ Melodic Minor Scale (Enharmonic of D♯ Melodic Minor)

Relative Minor of
G♭ Major

M.M. = 88 - 108

Ascending form only.

Descending form is
E♭ Natural Minor.

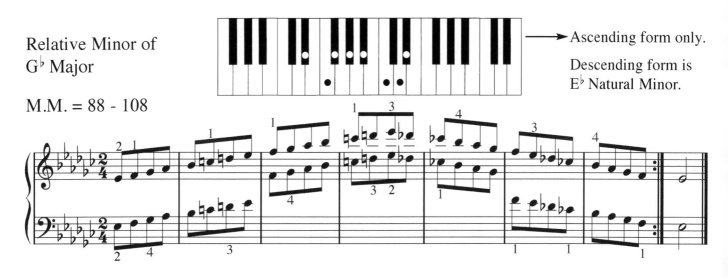

B♭ Melodic Minor Scale (Enharmonic of A♯ Melodic Minor)

Relative Minor of
D♭ Major

M.M. = 88 - 108

Ascending form only.

Descending form is
B♭ Natural Minor.

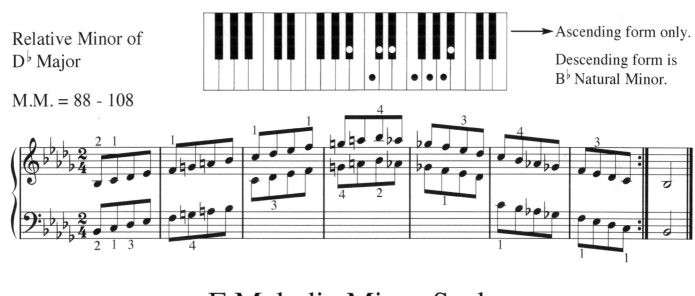

F Melodic Minor Scale

Relative Minor of
A♭ Major

M.M. = 88 - 108

Ascending form only.

Descending form is
F Natural Minor.

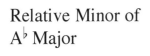
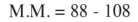
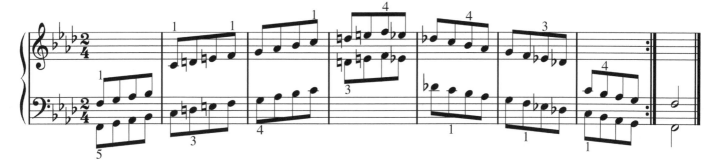

C Melodic Minor Scale

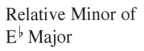

Relative Minor of
E♭ Major

M.M. = 88 - 108

→ Ascending form only.

Descending form is
C Natural Minor.

G Melodic Minor Scale

Relative Minor of
B♭ Major

M.M. = 88 - 108

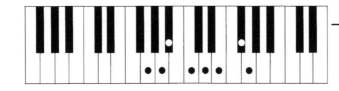

→ Ascending form only.

Descending form is
G Natural Minor.

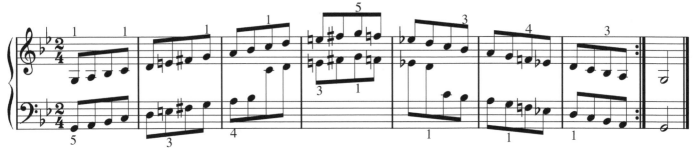

D Melodic Minor Scale

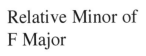

Relative Minor of
F Major

M.M. = 88 - 108

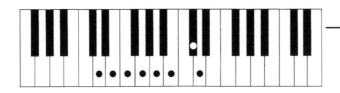

→ Ascending form only.

Descending form is
D Natural Minor.

Chromatic Scale
Parallel Motion

M.M. = 104 - 120

Parallel Motion - Legato Fingering

M.M. = 104 - 120

Supplemental: Play the chromatic scale in parallel motion at the intervallic distances shown below. Play these variations in two octaves using the non-legato fingering shown at the top of this page.

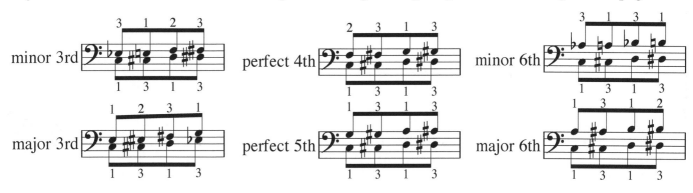

minor 3rd

perfect 4th

minor 6th

major 3rd

perfect 5th

major 6th

Contrary Motion - D Position

M.M. = 104 - 120

Contrary Motion - Legato Fingering

M.M. = 104 - 120

(can start on D position)

Supplemental: The number of variations for the chromatic scale in contrary motion is vast. Some common variations are given below. Try variations of your own.

at unison   at minor 3rd   at minor 6th   at major 6th

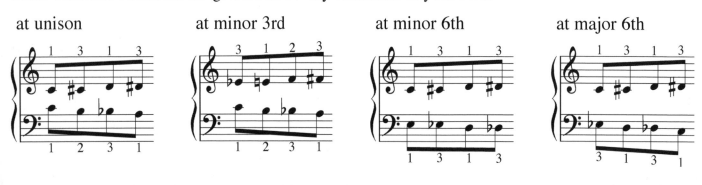

Whole Tone Scales

The whole tone scale is made up of six notes. Because it consists of successive whole steps, there are only two possible note combinations: (1) C, D, E, F♯, G♯ and A♯ or (2) C♯, D♯, F, G, A and B. The examples shown below, starting on C and C♯, demonstrate how each of the two scale patterns are played. The fingering stays the same for each note in each hand, regardless of the starting note. For example, the fingering for a whole tone scale starting on D would use finger 2 in each hand and progress through the remaining fingering sequence shown for C; a whole tone scale starting on E would use finger 1 in each hand and progress from there. (The same rule applies when using the scale that begins on C♯.) Start on any note and practice the correct fingering until the pattern is mastered.

M.M. = 88 - 108

Whole Tone Scale starting on C

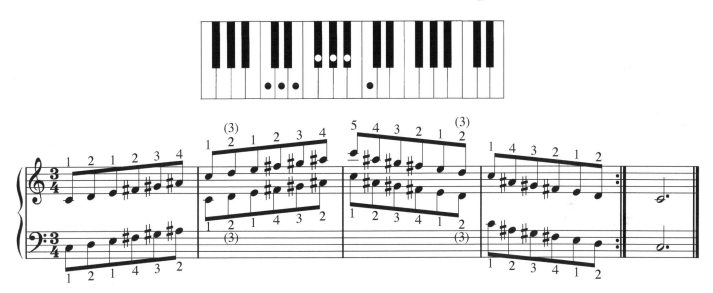

Whole Tone Scale starting on C♯

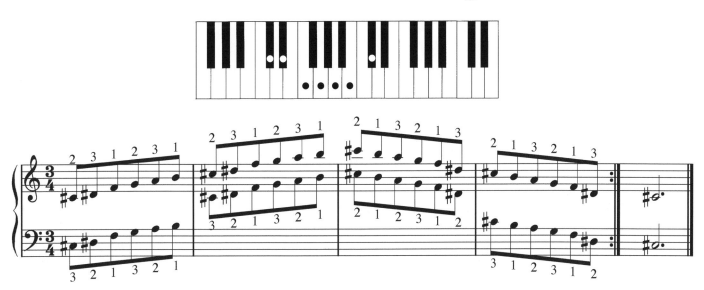

Modes of the C Major Scale

The modes are a series of scales derived from a "parent" scale. Each mode contains the same notes as the parent scale but in a different order, producing a new pattern of half and whole steps. Shown below are the seven modes derived from the major scale, in this case C Major. The major scale has the alternate mode name of Ionian, shown first below, but is rarely considered a "mode".

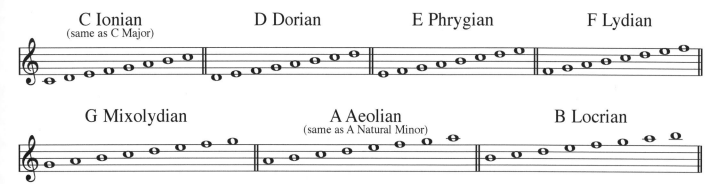

Notice how each mode starts with a sequential note from the parent scale. The new starting note gives rise to a new tonic name and thus a new tonality. D Dorian is a different tonality even though it has the same notes as C Major. The natural minor scales (now also known as the aeolian modes) were the first introduction to this concept.

The modes of C Major are presented below for study. The modes of other major scales may be studied as needed, adjusting fingering to prevent fingers 1 or 5 from striking black keys.

M.M. = 88 - 108

D Dorian
The second mode of C Major.

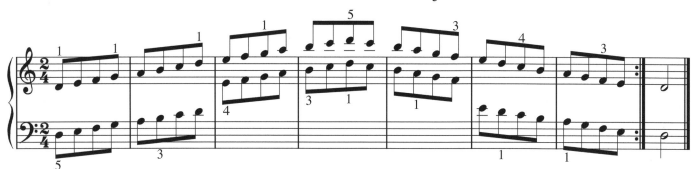

E Phrygian
The third mode of C Major.

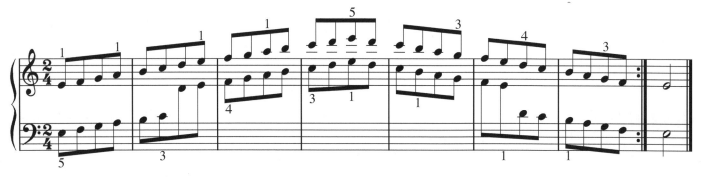

F Lydian
The fourth mode of C Major.

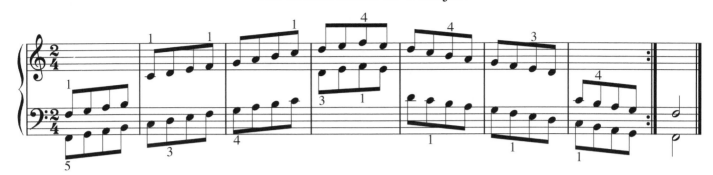

G Mixolydian
The fifth mode of C Major.

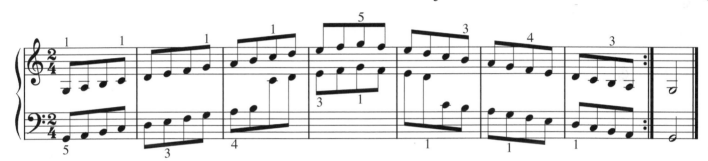

A Aeolian
The sixth mode of C Major.

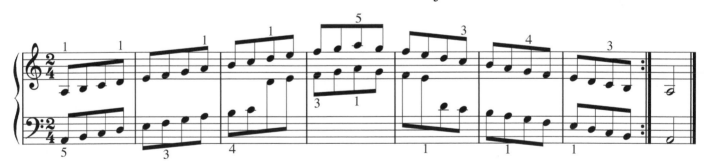

B Locrian
The seventh mode of C Major.

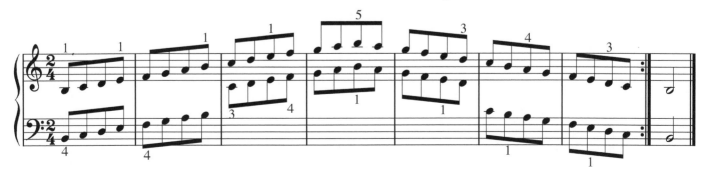

Scale Variations

To expand scale proficiency, keyboardists should practice scales using different rhythms, along with a variety of dynamics and articulations. This develops a masterful technique and keeps scale maintainence interesting over the years. The Scale Variations are presented in the key of C Major. Variations #2-11 require competence in all major keys. **Supplemental:** Apply these variations to all scale exercises.

1

Multiple Rhythms in C Major

Scale Variation #1 employs three different rhythms, from slowest to fastest and back to slowest. The R.H. is presented on a single staff. The L.H. is played one octave below the R.H. The dynamics and articulations to be used for *each rhythm* are shown in the first measure. Master these six individually. Then master each of the eight possible combinations of both. **Supplemental:** Mix and match the six individual and eight combinations of both *within the exercise.*

M.M. = 72 - 88

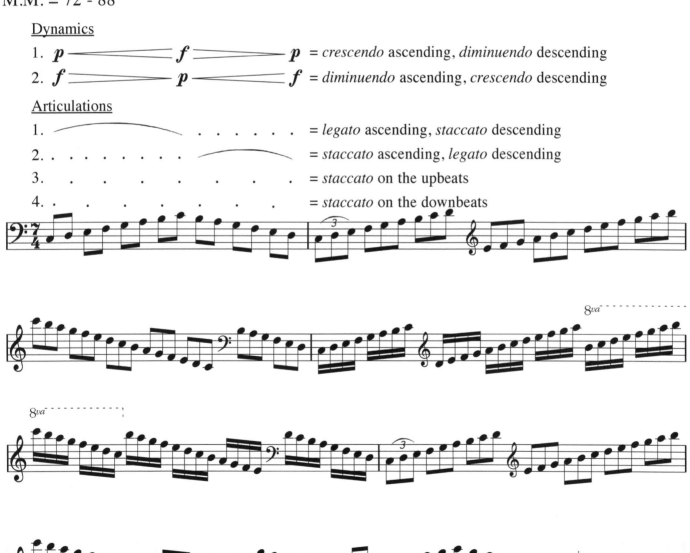

Dynamics

1. p ——————— f ——————— p = *crescendo* ascending, *diminuendo* descending
2. f ——————— p ——————— f = *diminuendo* ascending, *crescendo* descending

Articulations

1. ⌒ . . . . = *legato* ascending, *staccato* descending
2. . . . . ⌒ = *staccato* ascending, *legato* descending
3. . . . . = *staccato* on the upbeats
4. . . . . = *staccato* on the downbeats

Scale Variations #2-6 subdivide the beat with different note values. These variations improve rhythmic accuracy and increase agility in turning the wrist. Start slowly, gradually working up to the suggested tempo range. Once all five variations are mastered, switch rhythms at will within a three octave range. In doing so, the top and/or bottom notes may occur off the beat. This is not important. It is only necessary to keep the individual rhythms and the transitions between them precise, straight through to the end. Then master these variations in all major keys.

M.M. = 66 - 80

2

Eighth, Two Sixteenths

3

Two Sixteenths, Eighth

4

Sixteenth, Eighth, Sixteenth

5

Dotted Eighth, Sixteenth

6

Sixteenth, Dotted Eighth

7   Contrary and Parallel Motion

Scale Variation #7 alternates between movement in the same direction and movement in opposite directions. Learn this is in all major keys, maintaining correct scale fingering throughout.
Start slowly, gradually working up to the suggested tempo range.

Supplemental: Practice Scale Variation #7 using different dynamics and/or articulations. It is also an excellent exercise to play in thirds, as shown on pages 76-78, or other intervals such as sixths, fourths and fifths. Intervals other than the octave demand greater attention to fingering.

M.M. = 66 - 80

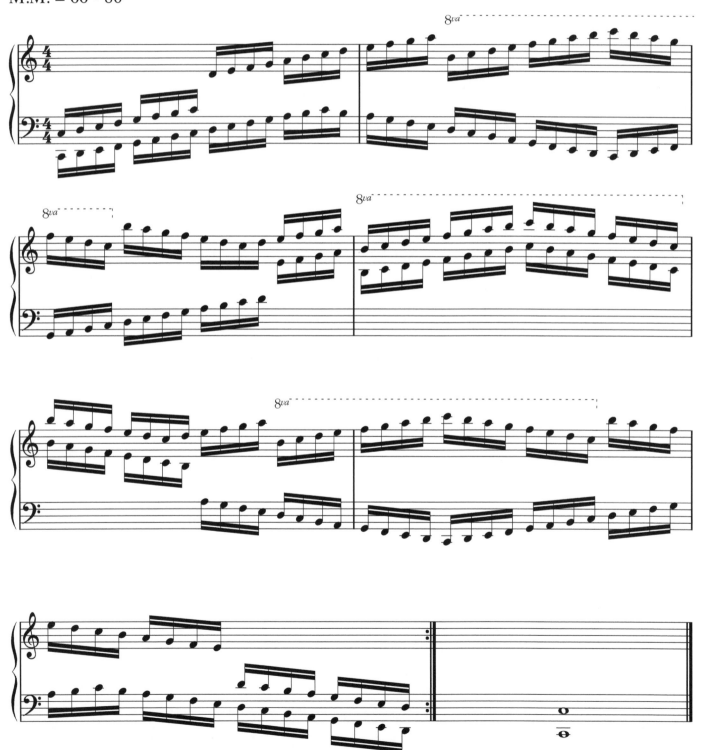

M.M. = 60 - 72

8   Alternating, Right-Left

9   Alternating, Right-Left, Legato

10   Alternating, Left-Right

11   Alternating, Left-Right, Legato

2:3 Polyrhythm Preparation #1

Pick two keys of the same name near the center of the keyboard. Practice 1A and 1B using every fingering combination listed below. For assistance coordinating two against three, see "Polyrhythms" in chapter 3 of **Piano Practice and Performance**.

Fingering Combinations

R.H. =	1	2	3	4	5	1	2	4	5
L.H. =	1	2	3	4	5	5	4	2	1

2:3 Polyrhythm Preparation #2

Practice 2A and 2B using each fingering combination below.

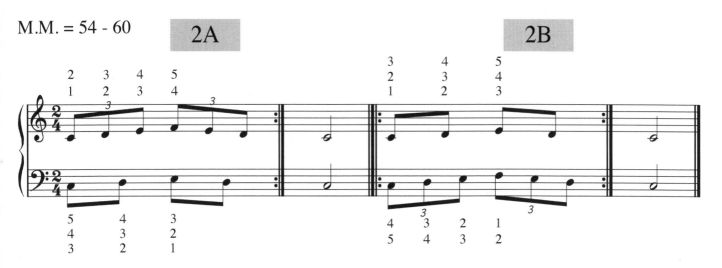

2:3 Polyrhythm - One Octave

Supplemental: Master these exercises in all major keys, maintaining correct scale fingering.

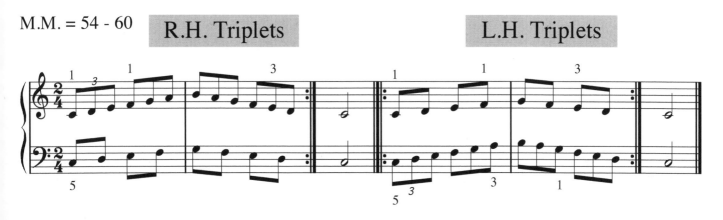

2:3 Polyrhythm - Three Octaves

Supplemental: Master these exercises in all major keys, maintaining correct scale fingering.

M.M. = 54 - 60

R.H. Triplets

L.H. Triplets

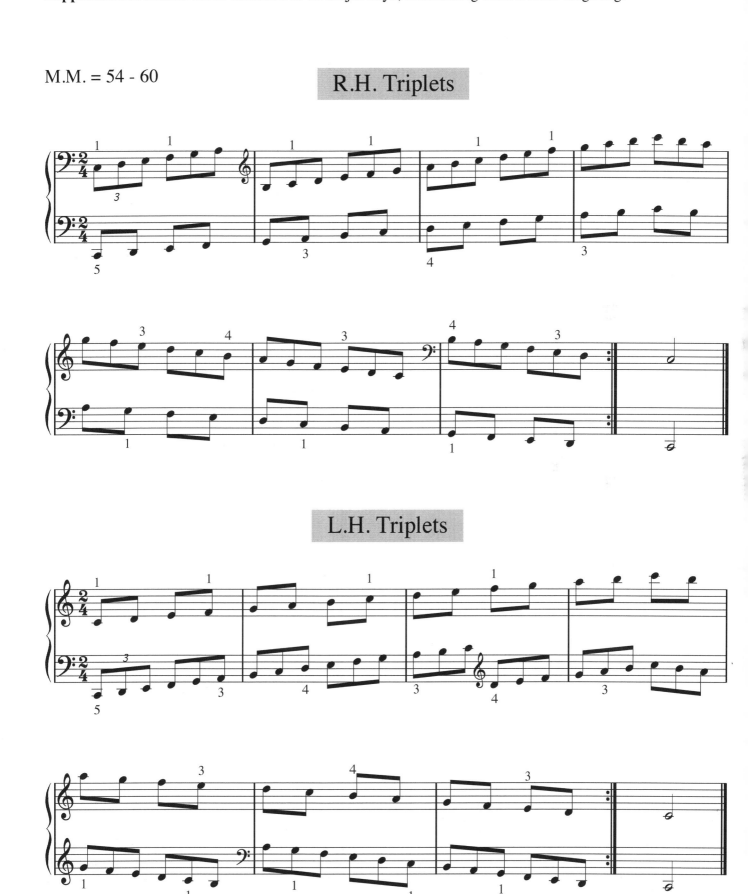

Major Scales in Thirds or Tenths

Practice the major scales in thirds as shown. When practicing tenths, L.H. plays one octave lower than written or R.H. plays one octave higher than written, whichever is preferred.

Supplemental: Practice the minor keys in this manner, keeping in mind the fingering which is accurate to each scale as well as possible adjustments to fingering at the top or bottom.

M.M. = 104 - 120

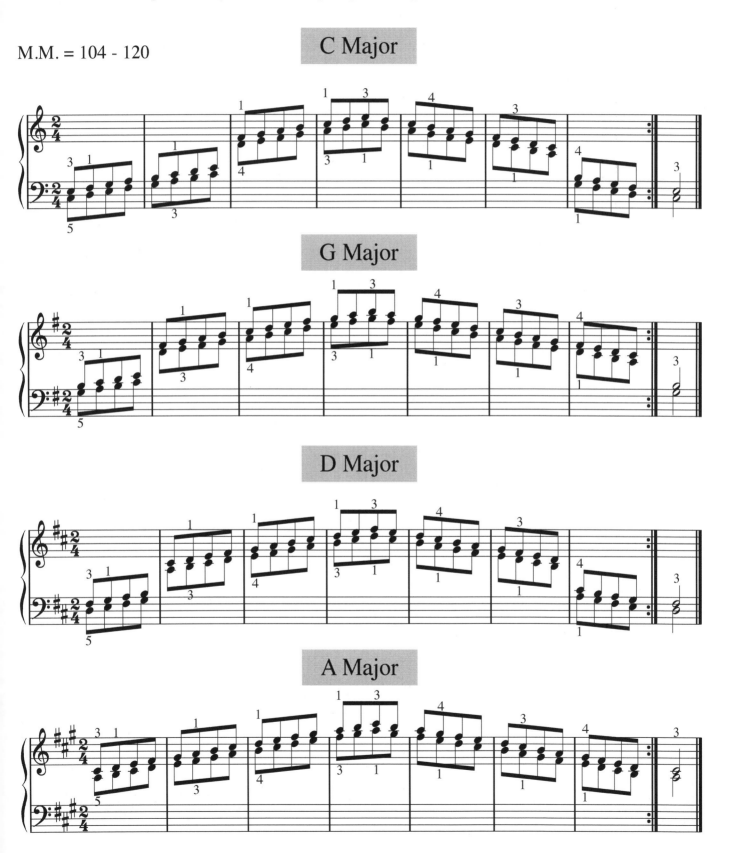

E Major

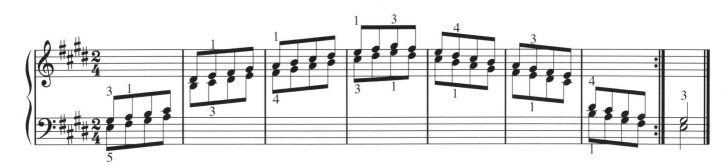

B Major

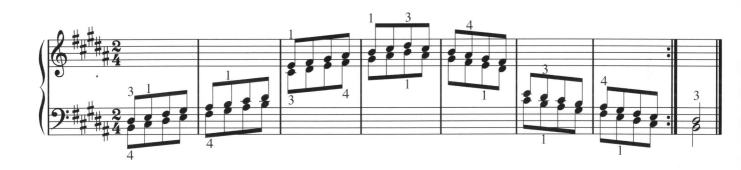

G♭ Major

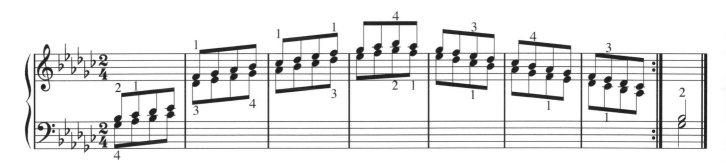

D♭ Major

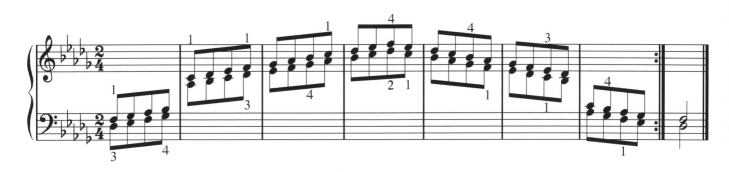

A♭ Major

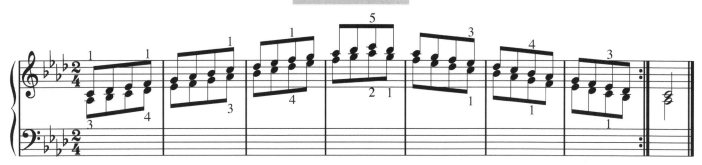

E♭ Major

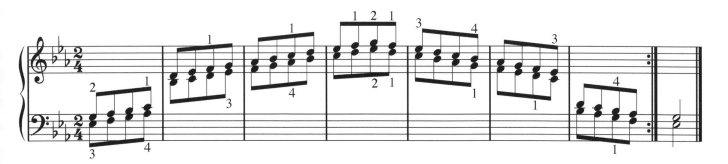

B♭ Major

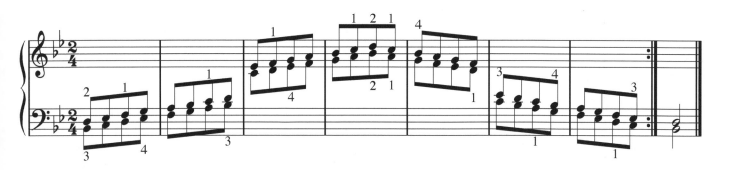

F Major

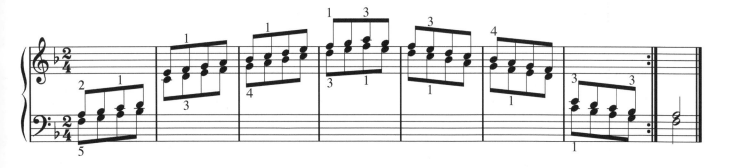

Major Scales in Sixths

Supplemental: Practice the minor keys in this manner, keeping in mind the fingering which is accurate to each scale as well as possible adjustments to fingering at the top or bottom.

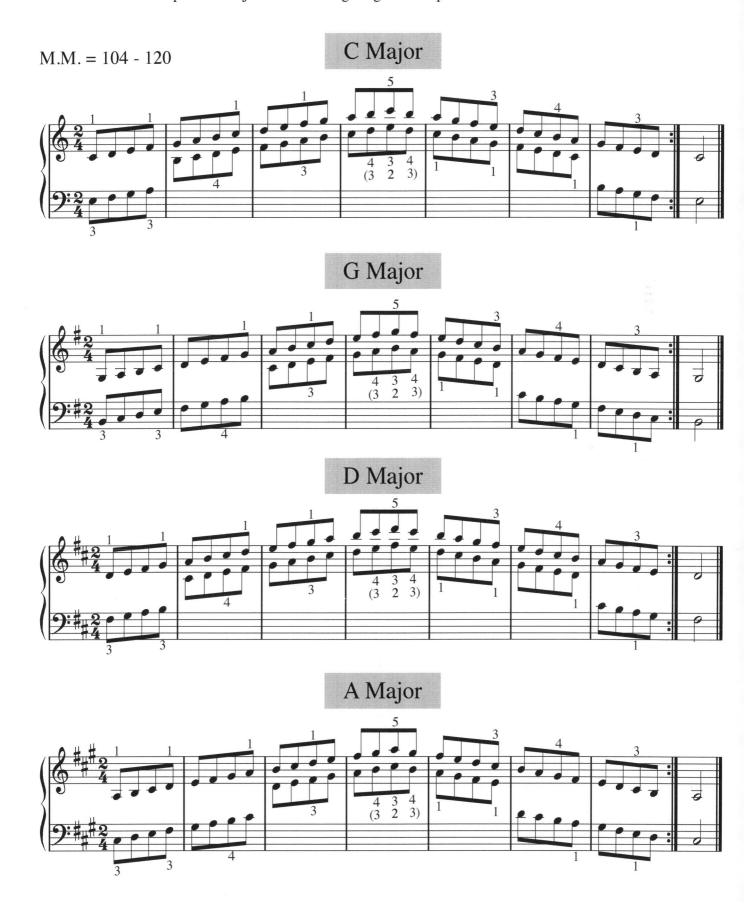

E Major

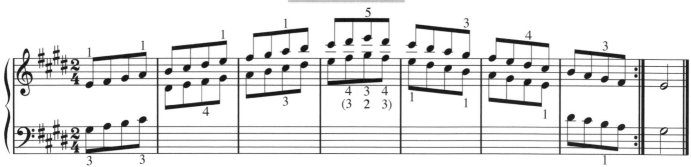

B Major

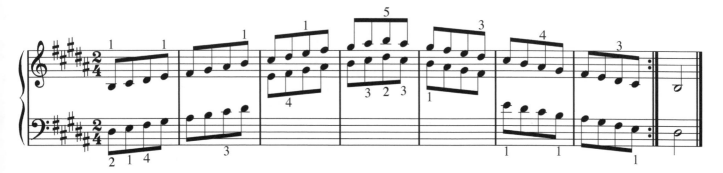

G♭ Major

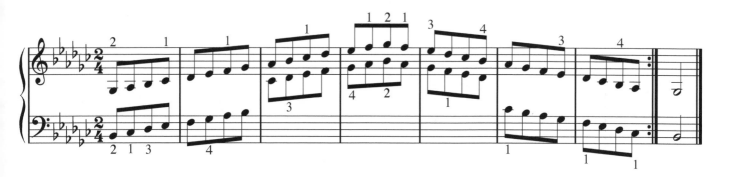

D♭ Major

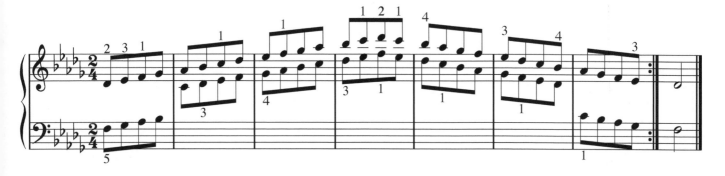

A♭ Major

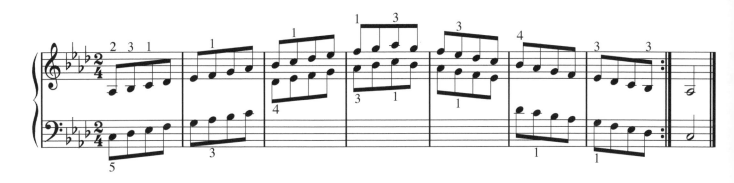

E♭ Major

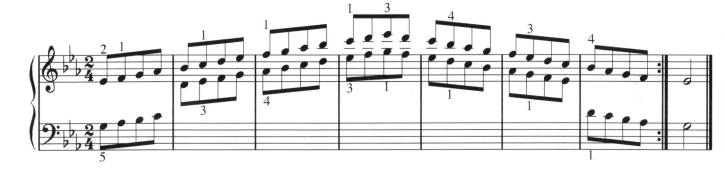

B♭ Major

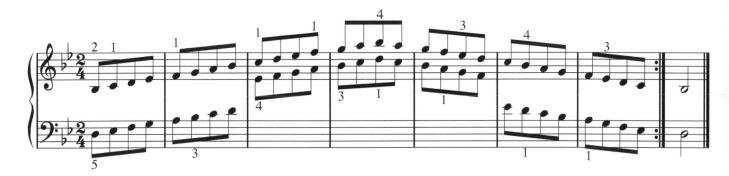

F Major

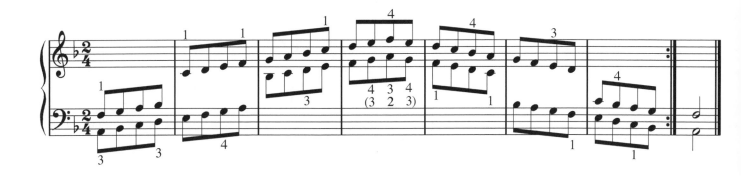

Scales in Octaves

The wrist remains loose and flexible during the up and down movement of each stroke. The fingertips maintain a slightly curved shape, especially in the unused fingers. The 1,5 fingering is used throughout, except in larger hands where a 1,4 fingering may be used on black keys in both hands. In either case, those fingertips remain firm. Keep the forearms relaxed to facilitate wrist strokes, reduce fatigue and accurately guide the hand-shape across the keyboard.

M.M. = 84 - 100

Chromatic Scale in Octaves

Major Scales in Octaves

M.M. = 84 - 100

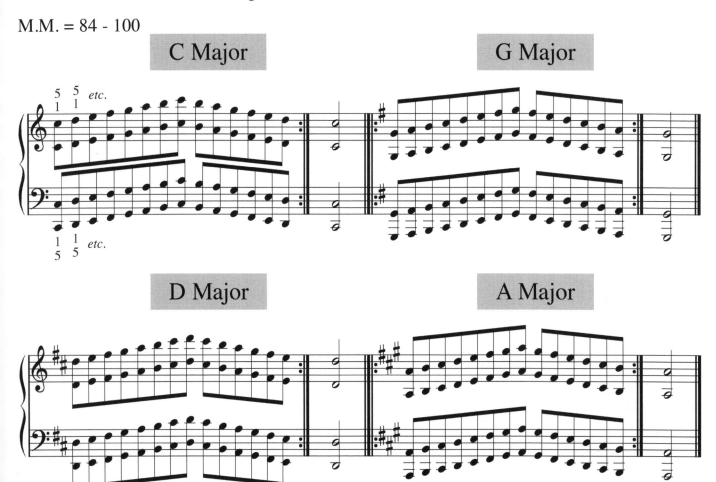

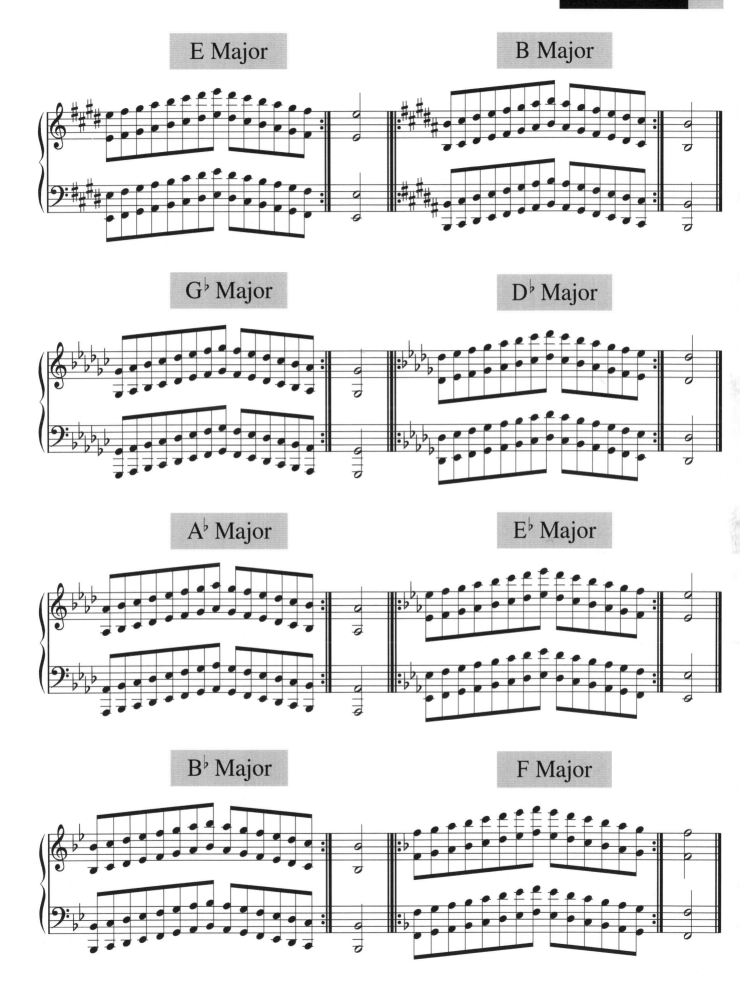

Harmonic Minor Scales in Octaves

R.H. fingering above, L.H. below. Play L.H. one octave below R.H.
Supplemental: Practice the natural and melodic minor scales in this manner.

M.M. = 84 - 100

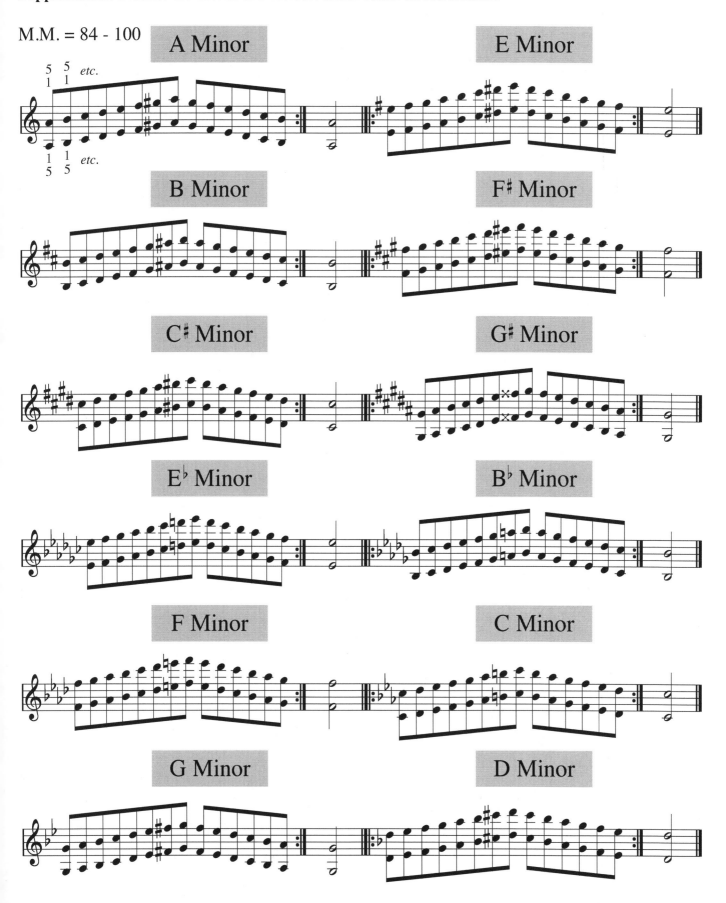

Major Scales in Broken Octaves #1-4

The wrist remains slightly taut as the forearm rotates back and forth, guiding the hands across the keyboard.
The fingertips maintain a slightly curved shape, especially in the unused fingers. The 1,5 fingering is used
throughout, except in larger hands, as previously noted. Each of the four patterns is presented in C Major.
Master these four patterns in every major key. **Supplemental:** Practice these in all minor keys.

M.M. = 100 - 116

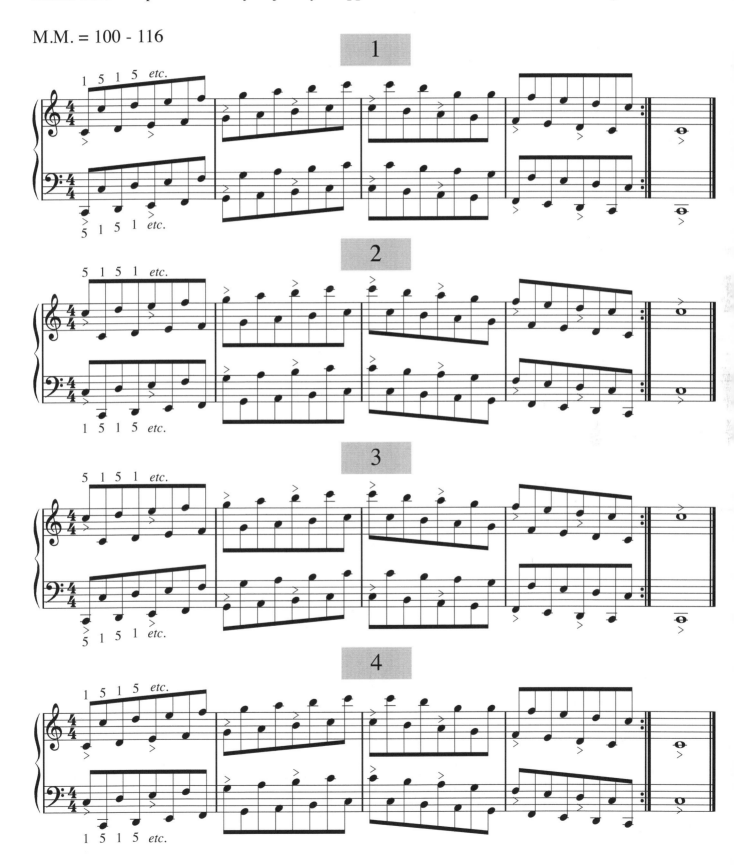

C Major Scale in Double Thirds - Staccato

The wrist remains loose and flexible during the up and down movement of each stroke, the fingertips held in a slightly curved position. Keep the forearms relaxed to facilitate wrist movement and reduce fatigue.
Supplemental: Practice all major scales using this fingering.

M.M. = 80 - 92

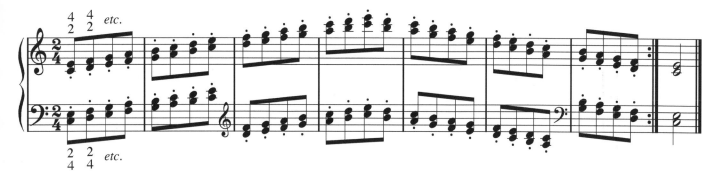

C Major Scale in Double Thirds - Legato

Shift hands quickly. This fingering could be used for any major or minor scale. Alternative fingerings can be found in the *Beringer Daily Technical Studies* or the *Hanon Virtuoso Pianist Book III*.

M.M. = 72 - 84

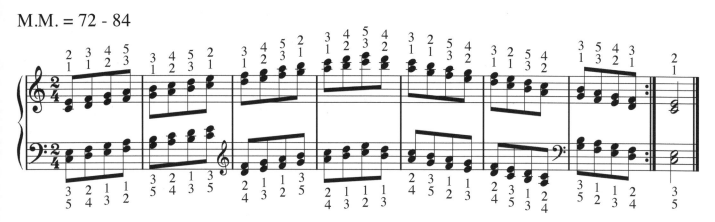

C Major Scale in Double Sixths - Staccato

See above comments for staccato double thirds. In practicing other scales, finger 4 may be used on black keys in place of finger 5. In either case, those fingertips remain firm. Keep the forearms relaxed in order to facilitate wrist strokes, reduce fatigue and accurately guide the hand-shape across the keyboard.

M.M. = 72 - 84

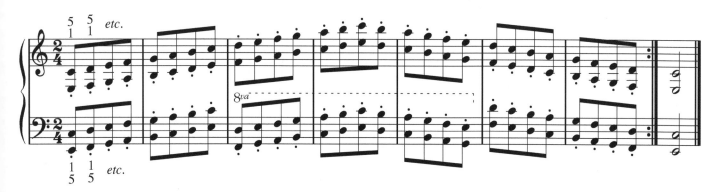

C Major Scale - Hand Over Hand

Either fingering may be used for each 3-note group, but avoid thumbs on black keys. Slide the hand toward you during each finger group to make way for the coming hand. **Supplemental:** Practice each line in all major scales.

M.M. = 96 - 108

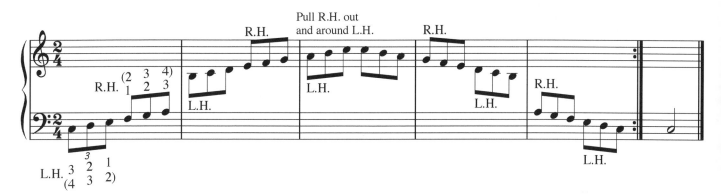

M.M. = 88 - 100

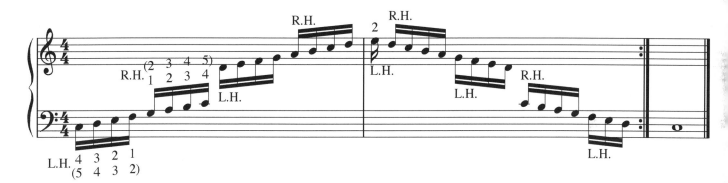

Essential Piano and Keyboard Technique

Section 3 Checksheet
Chords

✓	PROJECTS
☐	Major Triads - Blocked & Broken
☐	Minor Triads - Blocked & Broken
☐	Major Triads - Blocked & Broken - Octave Form
☐	Minor Triads - Blocked & Broken - Octave Form
☐	Major Triad Arpeggios
☐	Minor Triad Arpeggios
☐	Major Triads - Hand Over Hand
☐	Minor Triads - Hand Over Hand
☐	Dominant Seventh Tetrads (V^7) - Blocked & Broken
☐	Dominant Seventh Arpeggios
☐	Diminished Seventh Tetrads ($vii°^7$) - Blocked & Broken
☐	Diminished Seventh Arpeggios

Major Triads - Blocked & Broken

R.H. fingering above, L.H. below. Play L.H. one octave below R.H. Use the same fingering or alternatives (in parentheses) for all keys.

M.M. = 80 - 92

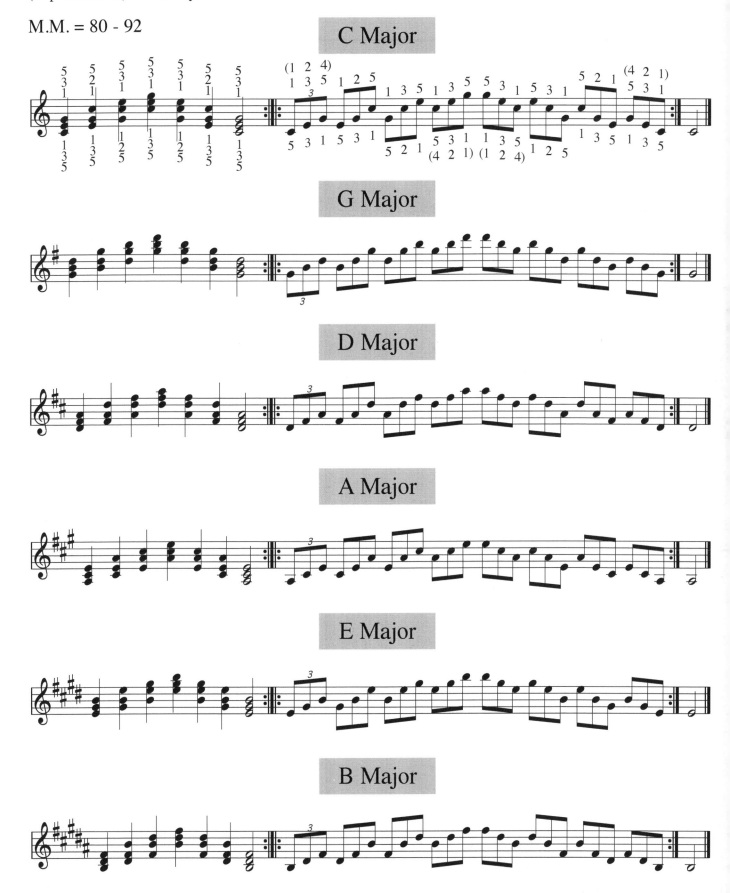

F♯ Major

D♭ Major

A♭ Major

E♭ Major

B♭ Major

F Major

Minor Triads - Blocked & Broken

R.H. fingering above, L.H. below. Play L.H. one octave below R.H. Use the same fingering or alternatives (in parentheses) for all keys.

M.M. = 80 - 92

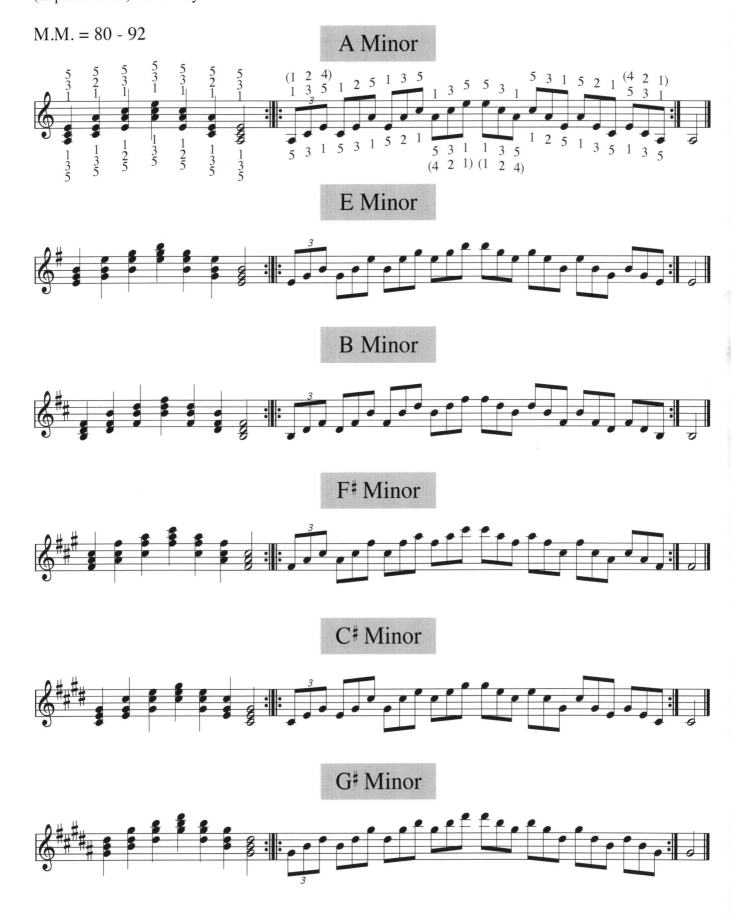

D♯ Minor

B♭ Minor

F Minor

C Minor

G Minor

D Minor

Major Triads - Blocked & Broken - Octave Form

Blocked triads are played two octaves apart. Broken triads are played one or two octaves apart.
Use the C Major fingering for all remaining keys. Alternate fingerings may be used, where indicated.

M.M. = 108 - 120

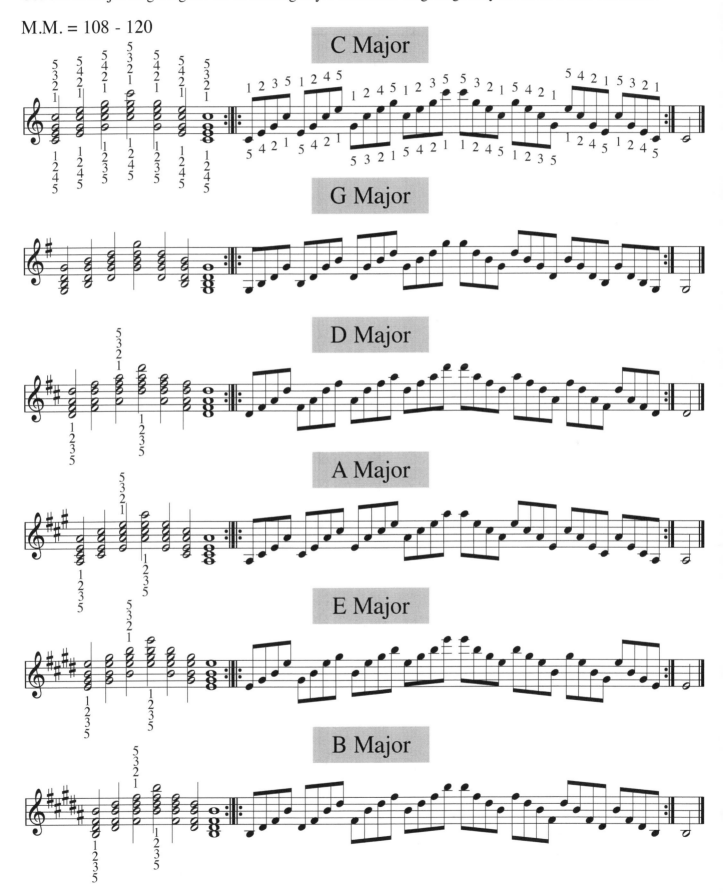

F♯ Major

D♭ Major

A♭ Major

E♭ Major

B♭ Major

F Major

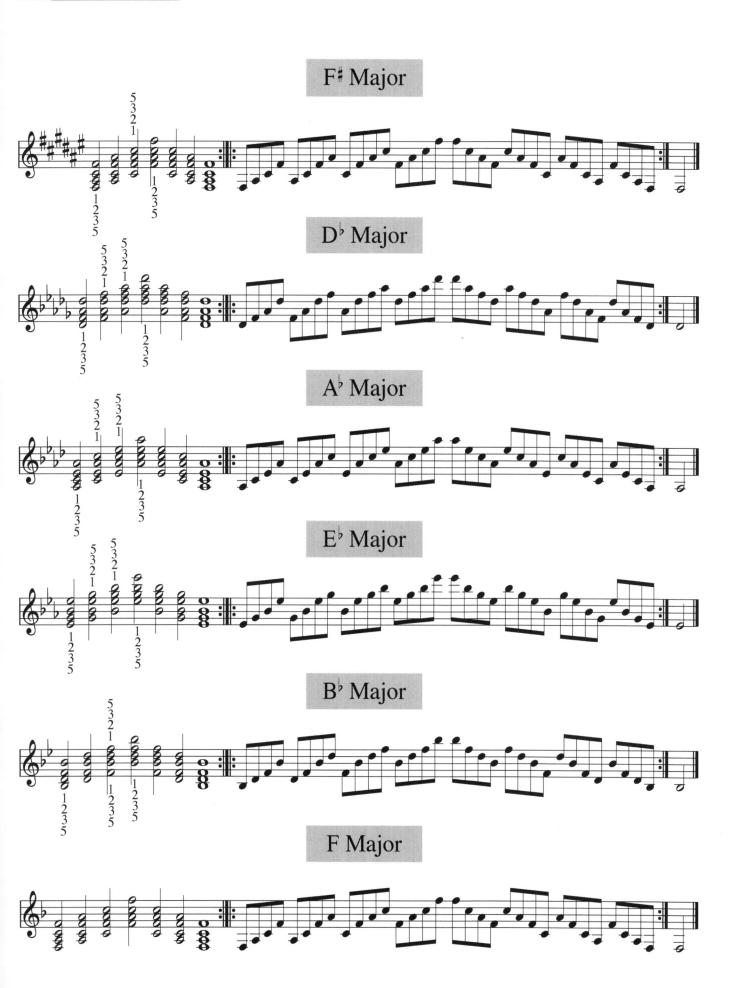

Minor Triads - Blocked & Broken - Octave Form

Blocked triads are played two octaves apart. Broken triads are played one or two octaves apart.
Use the A minor fingering for all remaining keys. Alternate fingerings may be used, where indicated.

M.M. = 108 - 120

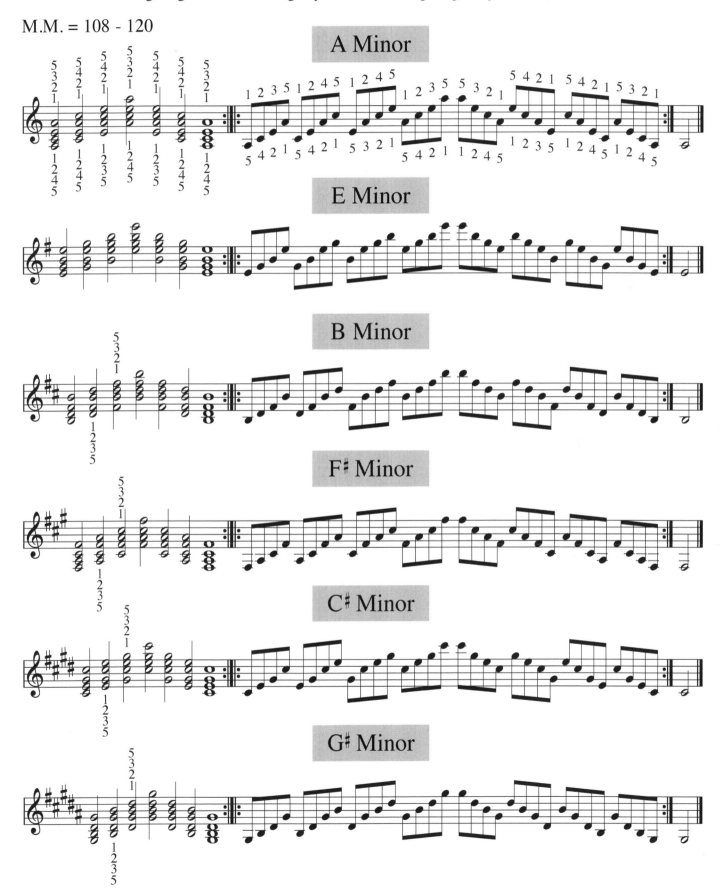

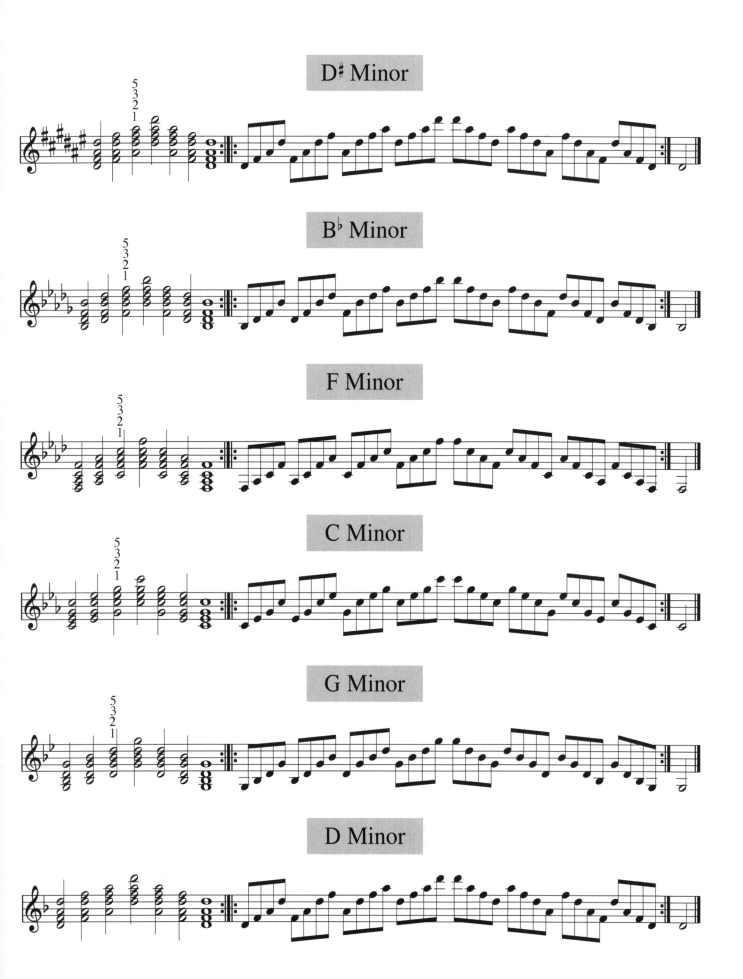

Major Triad Arpeggios

R.H. fingering above, L.H. below. Play L.H. one octave below R.H.

M.M. = 80 - 92 Play 4 times, then end.

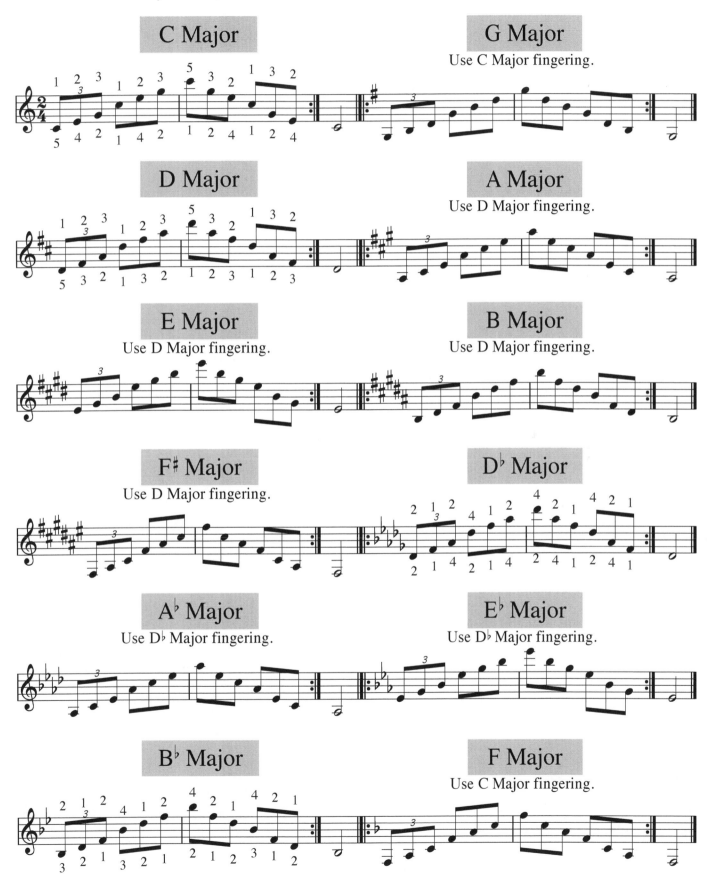

Minor Triad Arpeggios

R.H. fingering above, L.H. below. Play L.H. one octave below R.H.

M.M. = 80 - 92   Play 4 times, then end.

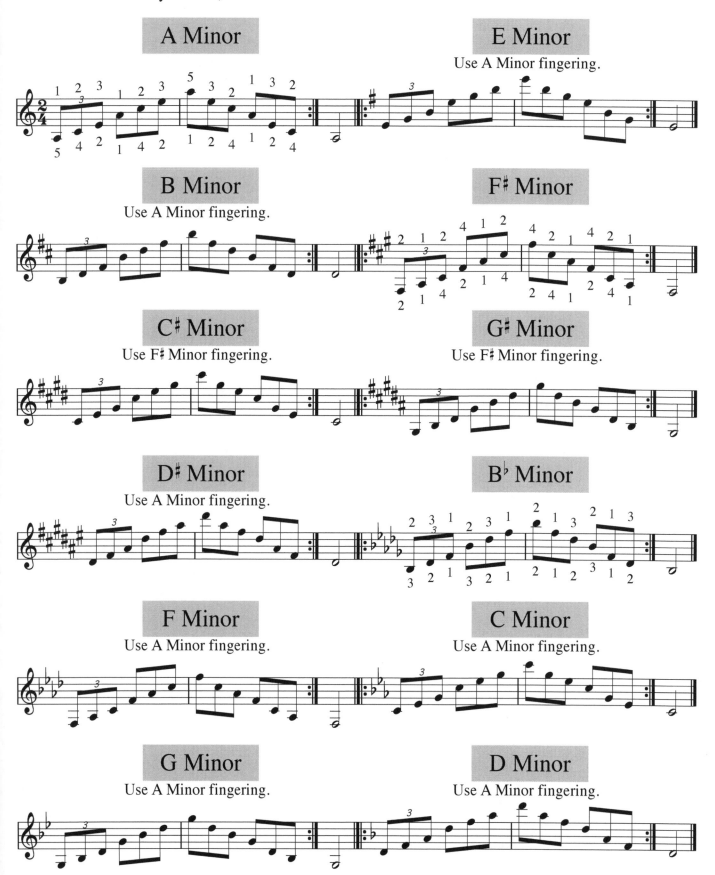

Major Triads - Hand Over Hand

Practice each line in all major keys. Use either of the fingerings in measure one, throughout.

Minor Triads - Hand Over Hand

Practice each line in all minor keys. Use either of the fingerings in measure one, throughout.

Dominant Seventh Tetrads (V⁷) - Blocked & Broken

R.H. fingering above, L.H. below. Play L.H. one octave below R.H. Use the C Major fingering or alternatives (in parentheses) for all keys.

M.M. = 108 - 120

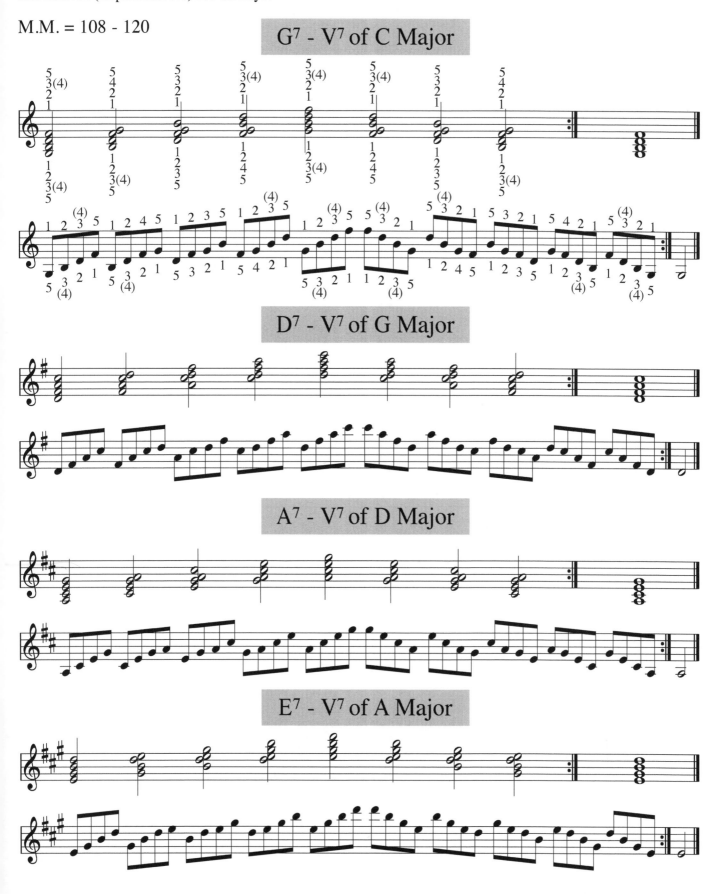

B⁷ - V⁷ of E Major

F♯⁷ - V⁷ of B Major

C♯⁷ - V⁷ of F♯ Major

A♭⁷ - V⁷ of D♭ Major

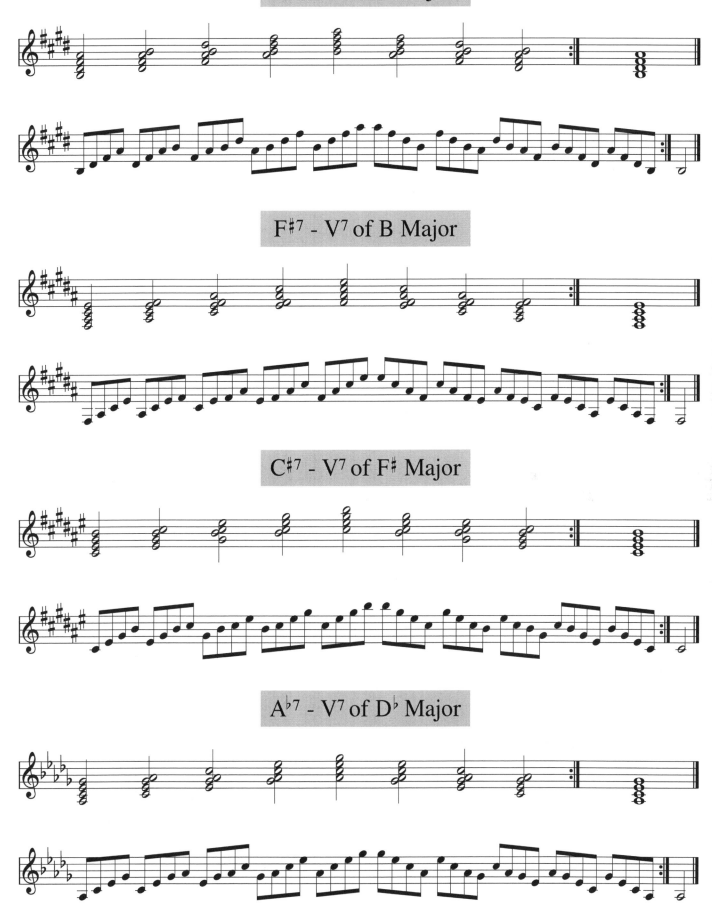

E♭7 - V7 of A♭ Major

B♭7 - V7 of E♭ Major

F7 - V7 of B♭ Major

C7 - V7 of F Major

Dominant Seventh Arpeggios

R.H. fingering above, L.H. below. Play L.H. one octave below R.H.

M.M. = 108 - 120 Play 4 times, then end.

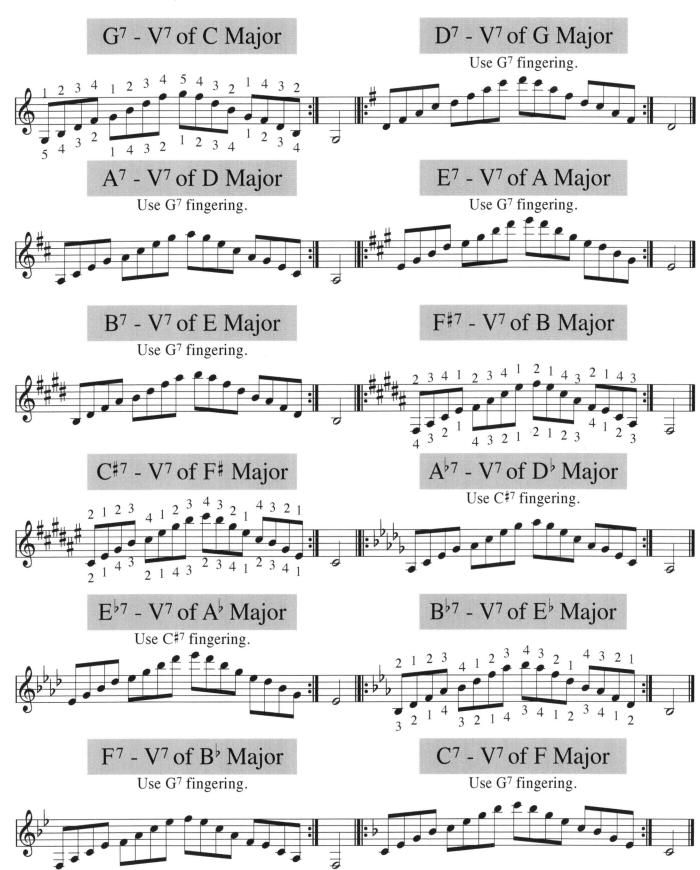

Diminished Seventh Tetrads (vii°7) - Blocked & Broken

R.H. fingering above, L.H. below. Play L.H. one octave below R.H. The consistent use of fingers 1, 2, 3, 5 in blocked form keeps the hand in a relaxed shape while developing visualization of diminished seventh chords.

Each inversion of a diminished seventh chord results in another diminished seventh chord with a different root. Thus, only three diminished seventh chords and their "inversions" are necessary for blocked and broken study of all twelve diminished seventh chords. The chosen keys of C, C♯ and D minor are presented below.

M.M. = 108 - 120

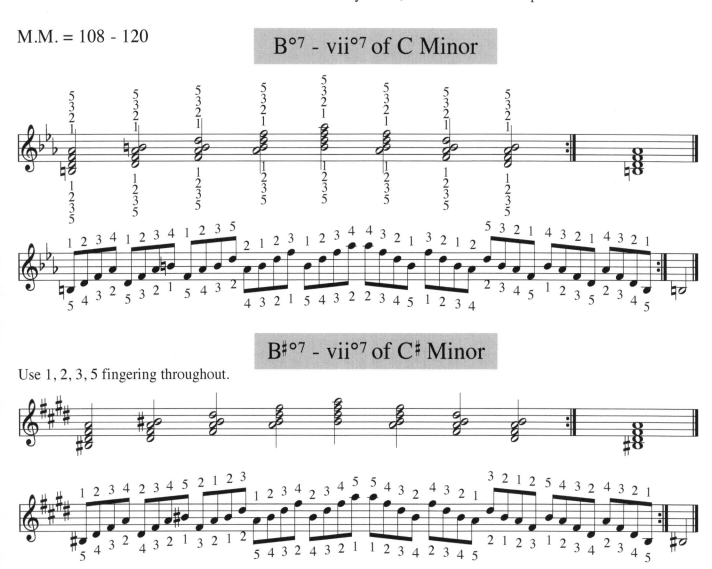

B°7 - vii°7 of C Minor

B♯°7 - vii°7 of C♯ Minor

Use 1, 2, 3, 5 fingering throughout.

C♯°7 - vii°7 of D Minor

Use 1, 2, 3, 5 fingering throughout.

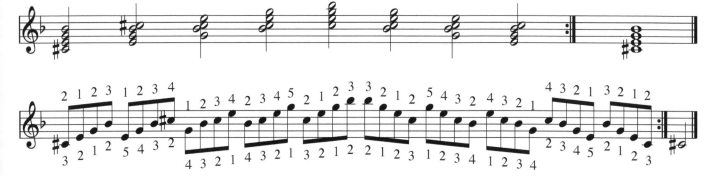

Diminished Seventh Arpeggios

R.H. fingering above, L.H. below. Play L.H. one octave below R.H.

M.M. = 108 - 120 Play 4 times, then end.

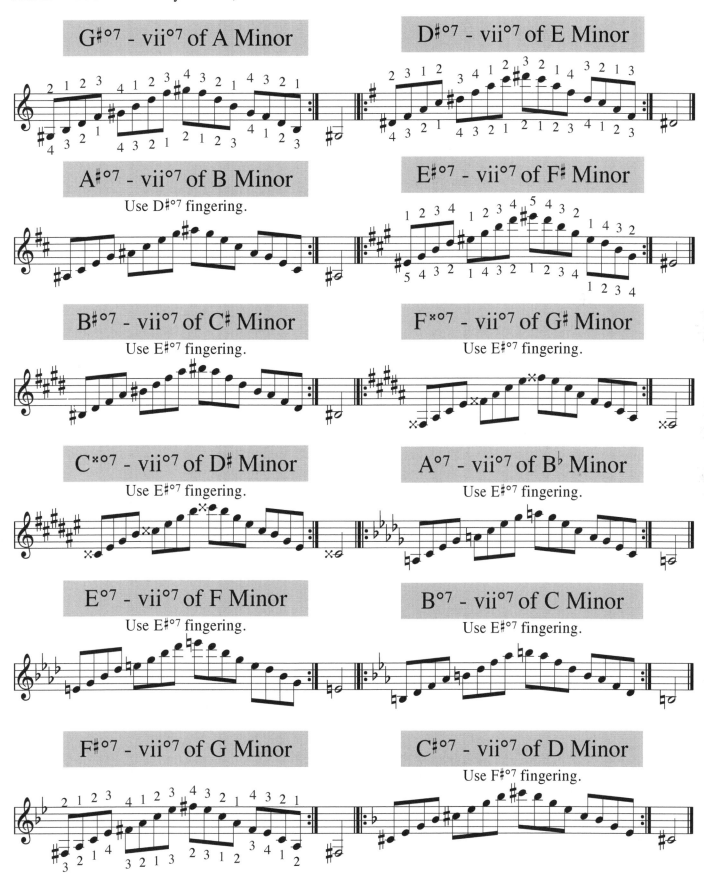

Essential Piano and Keyboard Technique

Section 4 Checksheet
Chord Progressions & Cadences

✓	**PROJECTS**
☐	Diatonic Triads - Major
☐	Diatonic Triads - Harmonic Minor
☐	Diatonic Triads - Ascending (Jazz) Melodic Minor
☐	I-V-I Progressions
☐	Cadences
☐	I-IV-I-V-V^7-I Progression - All Positions
☐	i-iv-i-V-V^7-i Progression - All Positions
☐	I-IV-ii-V^7-I Progression - All Positions
☐	I-iv-ii°-V^7-i Progression - All Positions
☐	I-IV-ii-V^7-vi Progression - All Positions
☐	I-iv-ii°-V^7-VI Progression - All Positions
☐	I-vi-IV-ii-I-V^7-I Progression - All Positions
☐	V^7/IV Secondary Dominant Progression - All Positions
☐	V^7/V Secondary Dominant Progression - All Positions
☐	Modulation to the Dominant Progression

Regimen for Chord Progressions & Cadences

• Practice hands separately, then together.
• Memorize each key before continuing to the next.
Supplemental: When not presented, derive first and second inversions as a visual and aural exercise.
At a slower pace, name the chords while playing, as in "C Major, D minor, E minor..." for C Major, below.

Diatonic Triads - Major

Use 1, 3, 5 or 1, 2, 4 fingering at suitable points through the series of chords. Play each series up and down.

M.M. = 92 - 108

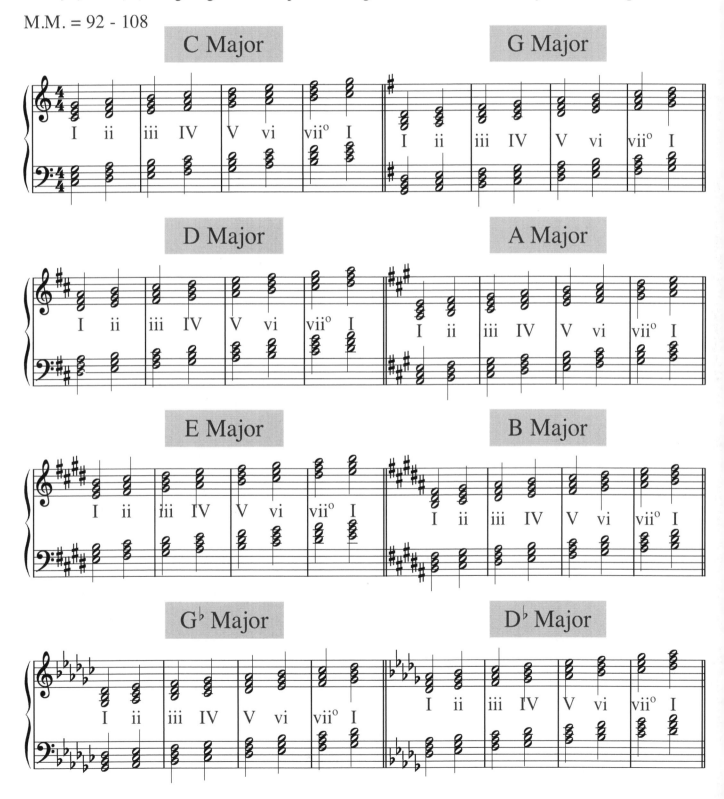

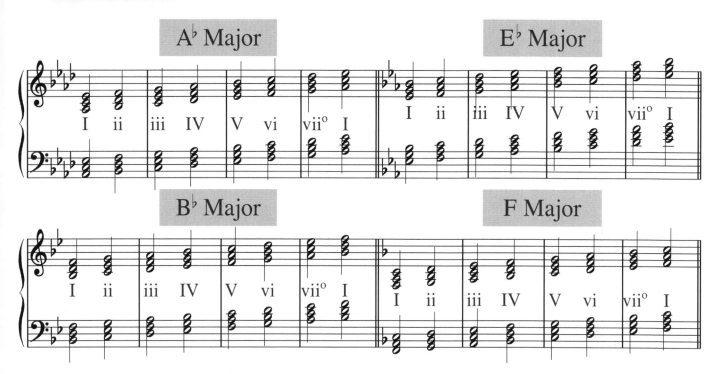

Diatonic Triads - Harmonic Minor

Use 1, 3, 5 or 1, 2, 4 fingering at suitable points through the series of chords. Play each series of triads up and back down.

M.M. = 92 - 108

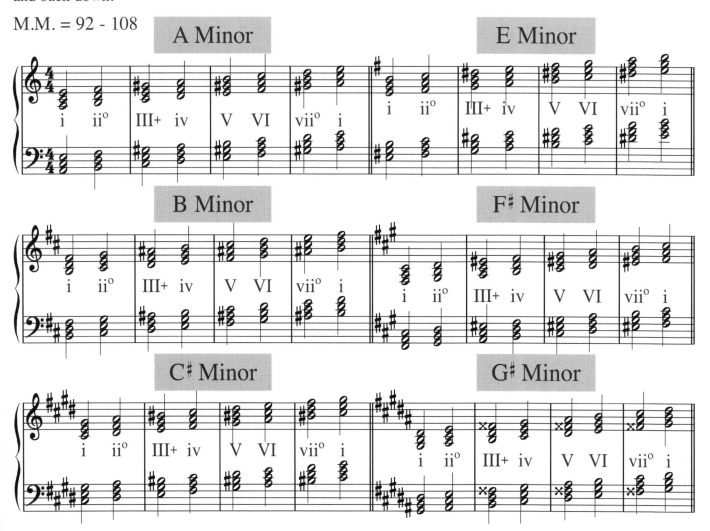

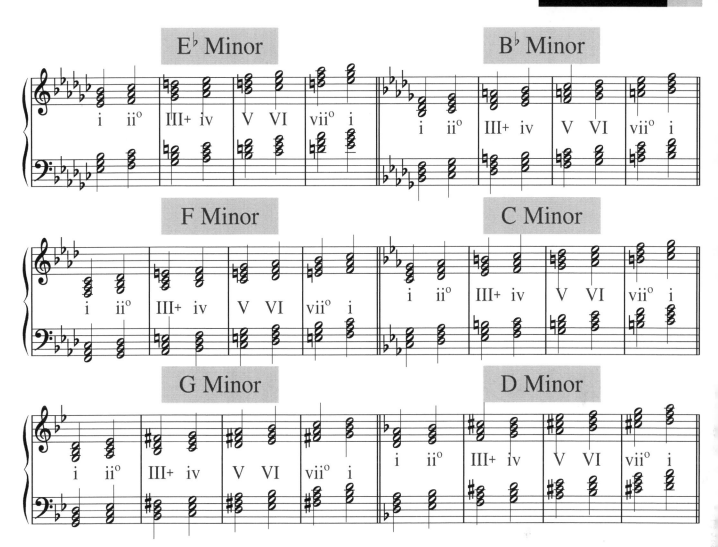

Diatonic Triads - Ascending (Jazz) Melodic Minor

Use 1, 3, 5 or 1, 2, 4 fingering at suitable points through the series of chords. Play each series of triads up and back down.

M.M. = 92 - 108

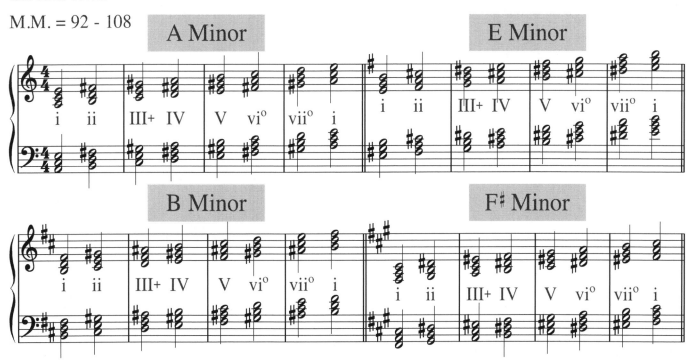

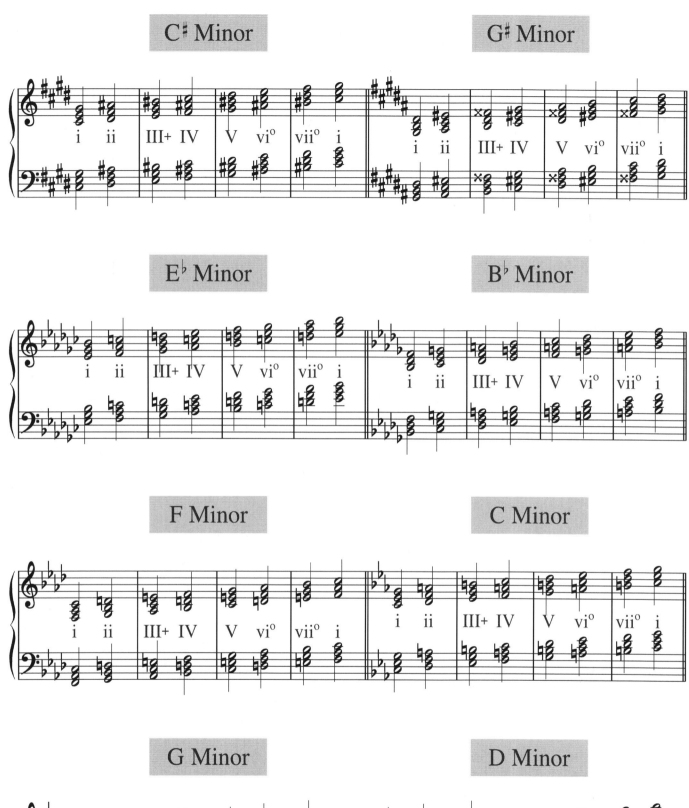

I-V-I Progressions

The fingering shown below is recommended to develop the greatest efficiency in the hands. It can be used in all major keys.

M.M. = 92 - 108

E Major

Root Position   Common Tone Inversions   Common tone is B.

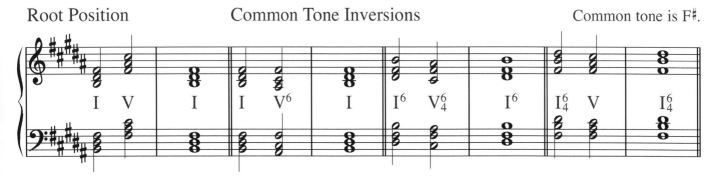

B Major

Root Position   Common Tone Inversions   Common tone is F♯.

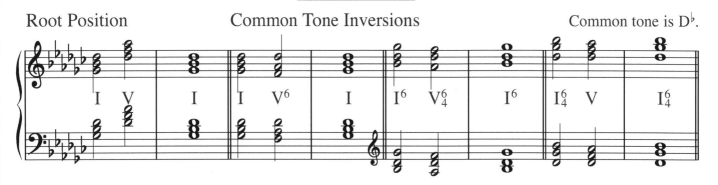

G♭ Major

Root Position   Common Tone Inversions   Common tone is D♭.

D♭ Major

Root Position   Common Tone Inversions   Common tone is A♭.

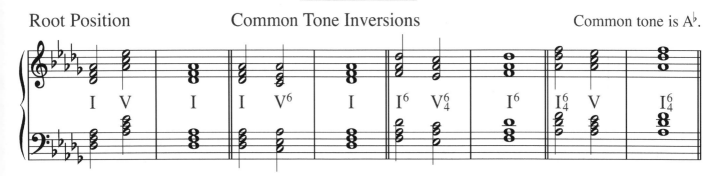

A♭ Major

Root Position   Common Tone Inversions   Common tone is E♭.

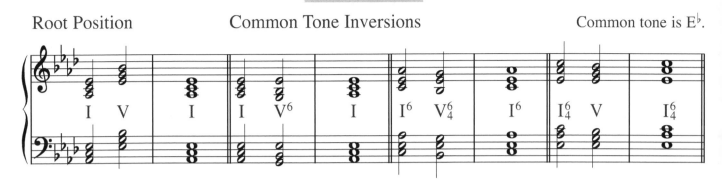

E♭ Major

Root Position   Common Tone Inversions   Common tone is B♭.

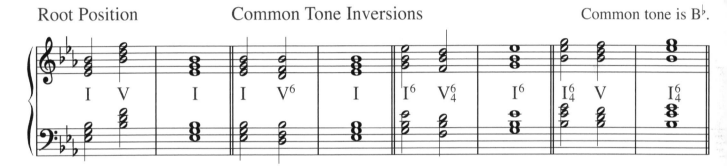

B♭ Major

Root Position   Common Tone Inversions   Common tone is F.

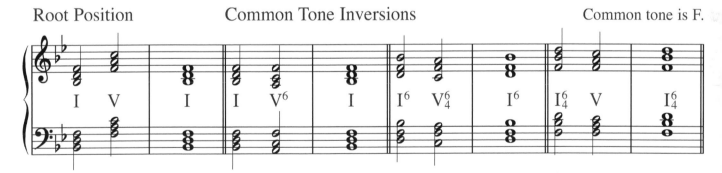

F Major

Root Position   Common Tone Inversions   Common tone is C.

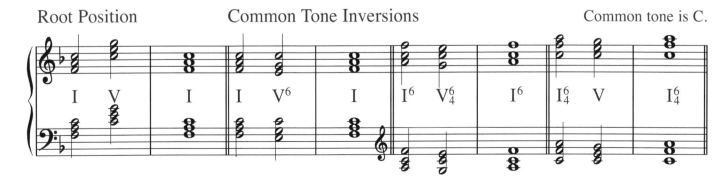

Cadences

With the exception of the IV-V half cadence, common tones are used to demonstrate effective voice leading. Other common tone movements exist, both here and in subsequent studies, but those presented in this book are the ones typically found in state and national examinations. Use the fingering below for all keys.

M.M. = 92 - 108

C Major

G Major

D Major

A Major

E Major

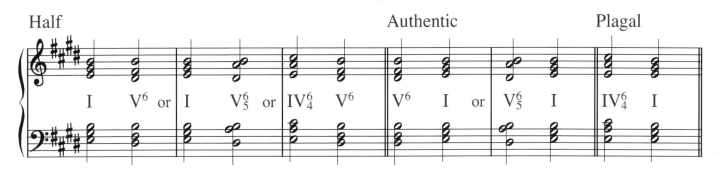

B Major

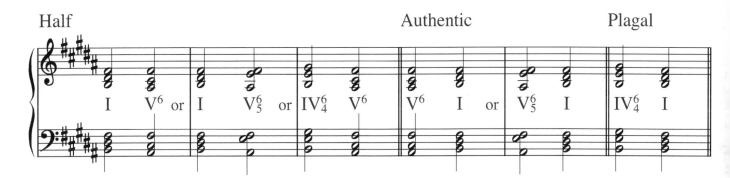

G♭ Major

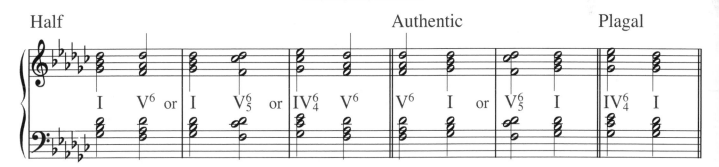

D♭ Major

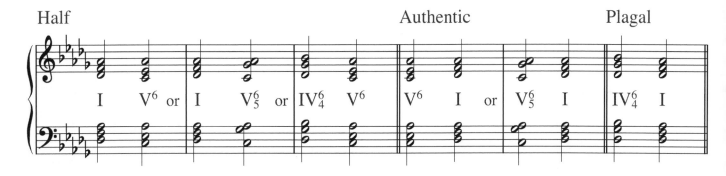

A♭ Major

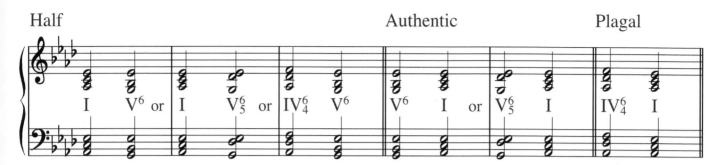

E♭ Major

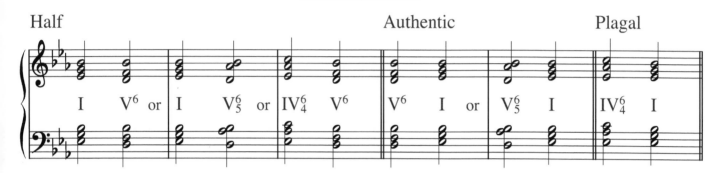

B♭ Major

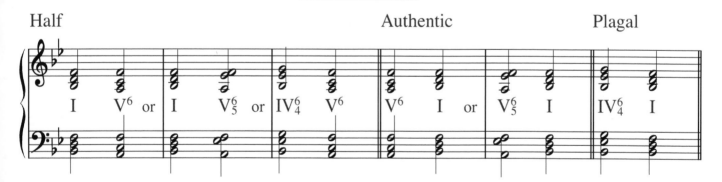

F Major

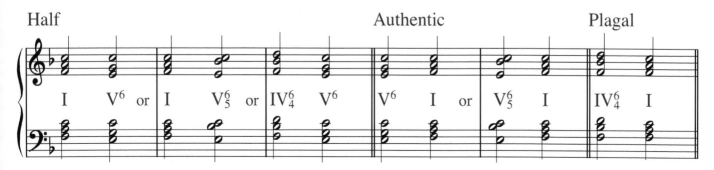

I-IV-I-V-V⁷-I Progression - All Positions

Use the C Major fingering for all keys. When ready, add legato pedaling to all progressions. Either of the two V chords may be practiced, or both.

M.M. = 92 - 108

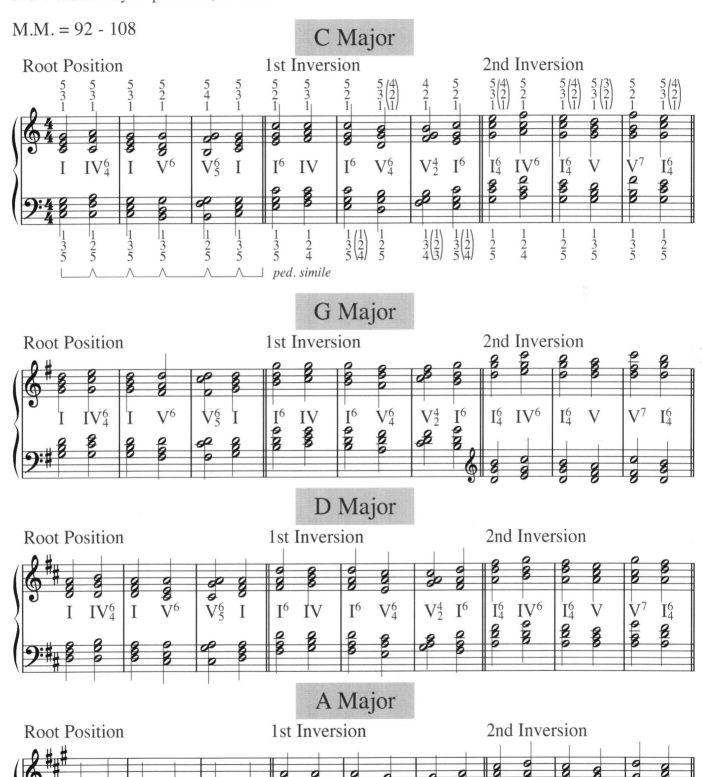

E Major

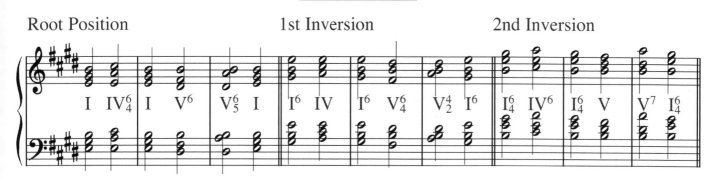

B Major

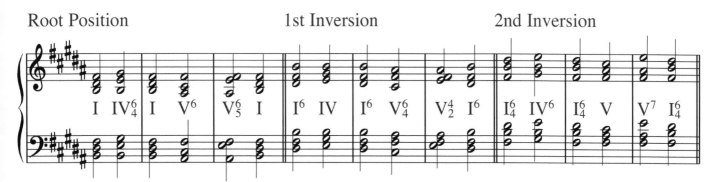

G♭ Major

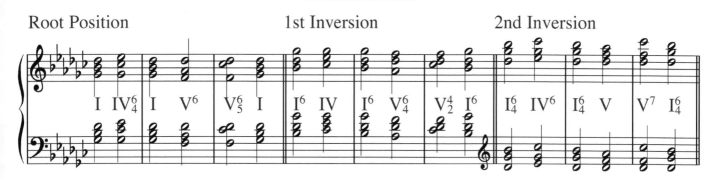

D♭ Major

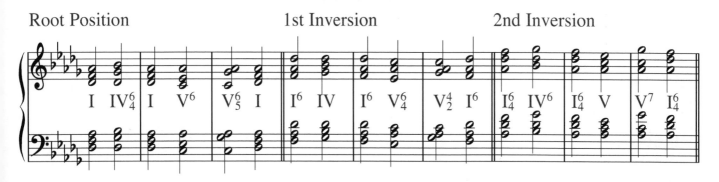

A♭ Major

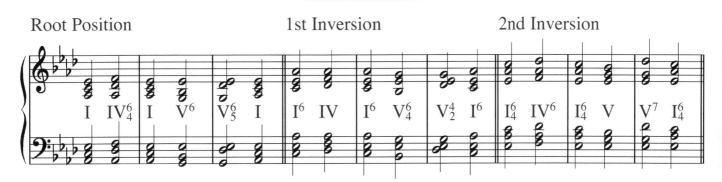

E♭ Major

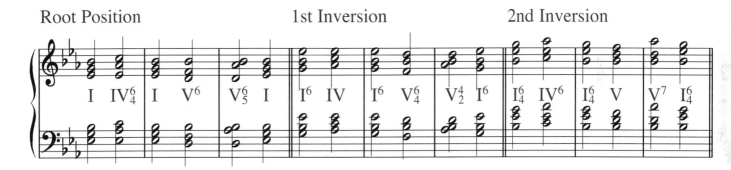

B♭ Major

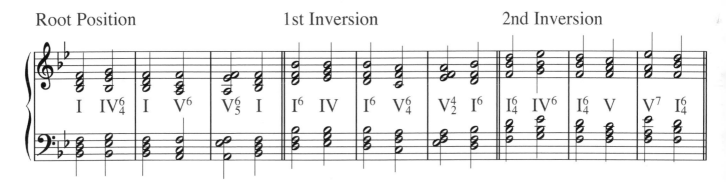

F Major

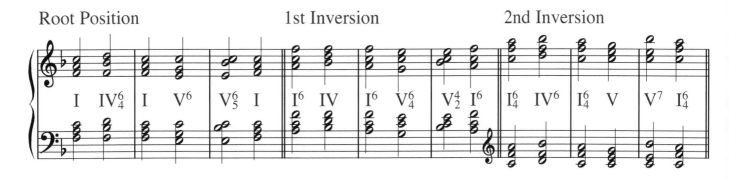

i-iv-i-V-V⁷-i Progression - All Positions

Use the A harmonic minor fingering for all keys. Either of the two V chords may be practiced, or both.

M.M. = 92 - 108

A Minor

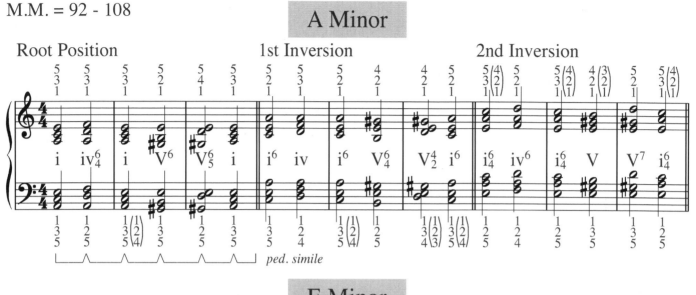

Root Position · 1st Inversion · 2nd Inversion

ped. simile

E Minor

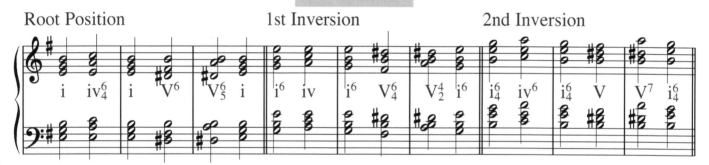

Root Position · 1st Inversion · 2nd Inversion

B Minor

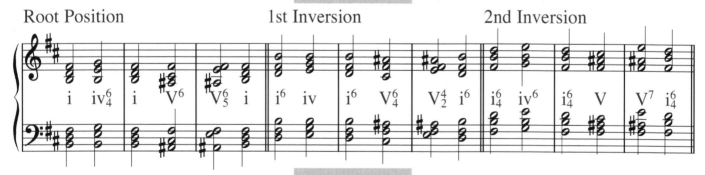

Root Position · 1st Inversion · 2nd Inversion

F♯ Minor

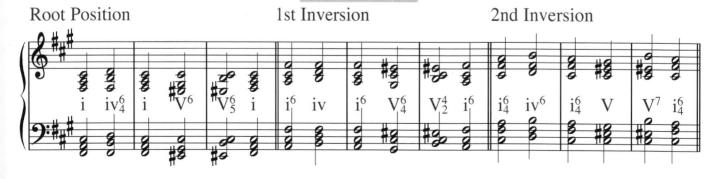

Root Position · 1st Inversion · 2nd Inversion

C♯ Minor

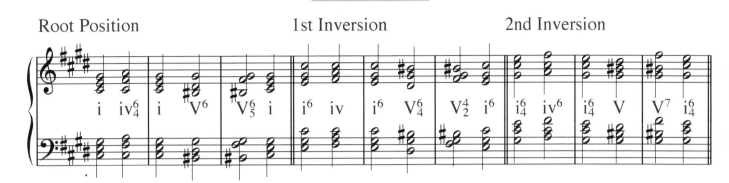

G♯ Minor

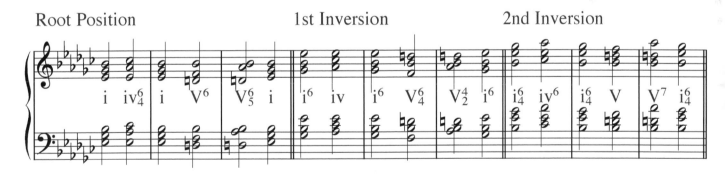

E♭ Minor

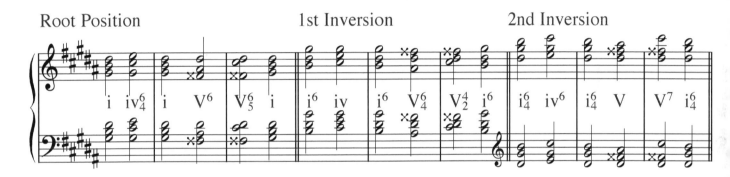

B♭ Minor

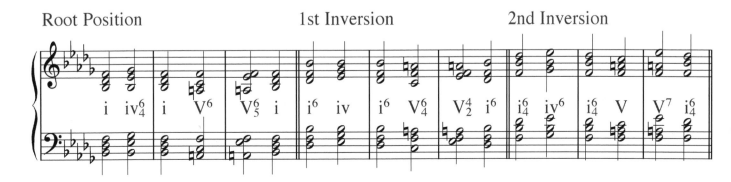

F Minor

Root Position   1st Inversion   2nd Inversion

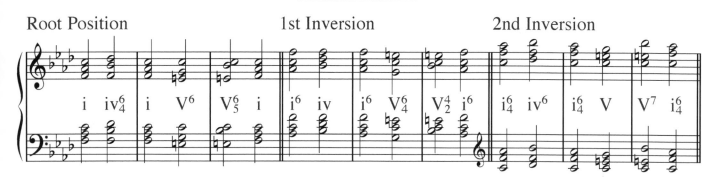

$$ i \quad iv^6_4 \quad i \quad V^6 \quad V^6_5 \quad i \quad \| \quad i^6 \quad iv \quad i^6 \quad V^6_4 \quad V^4_2 \quad i^6 \quad \| \quad i^6_4 \quad iv^6 \quad i^6_4 \quad V \quad V^7 \quad i^6_4 $$

C Minor

Root Position   1st Inversion   2nd Inversion

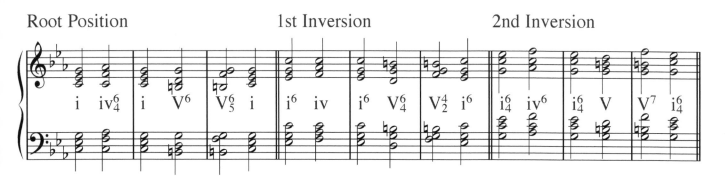

$$ i \quad iv^6_4 \quad i \quad V^6 \quad V^6_5 \quad i \quad \| \quad i^6 \quad iv \quad i^6 \quad V^6_4 \quad V^4_2 \quad i^6 \quad \| \quad i^6_4 \quad iv^6 \quad i^6_4 \quad V \quad V^7 \quad i^6_4 $$

G Minor

Root Position   1st Inversion   2nd Inversion

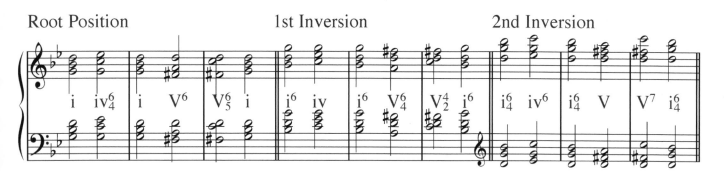

$$ i \quad iv^6_4 \quad i \quad V^6 \quad V^6_5 \quad i \quad \| \quad i^6 \quad iv \quad i^6 \quad V^6_4 \quad V^4_2 \quad i^6 \quad \| \quad i^6_4 \quad iv^6 \quad i^6_4 \quad V \quad V^7 \quad i^6_4 $$

D Minor

Root Position   1st Inversion   2nd Inversion

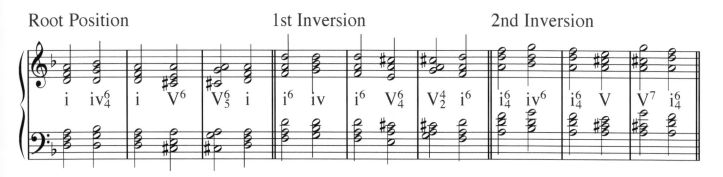

$$ i \quad iv^6_4 \quad i \quad V^6 \quad V^6_5 \quad i \quad \| \quad i^6 \quad iv \quad i^6 \quad V^6_4 \quad V^4_2 \quad i^6 \quad \| \quad i^6_4 \quad iv^6 \quad i^6_4 \quad V \quad V^7 \quad i^6_4 $$

I-IV-ii-V⁷-I Progression - All Positions

Use the C Major fingering for all keys. Practice each position separately before combining all three together in sequence.

M.M. = 92 - 108

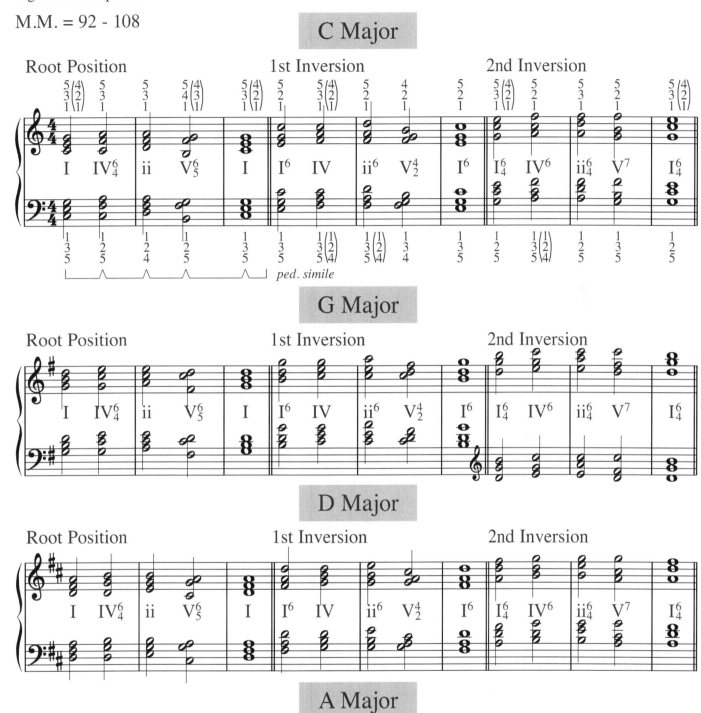

E Major

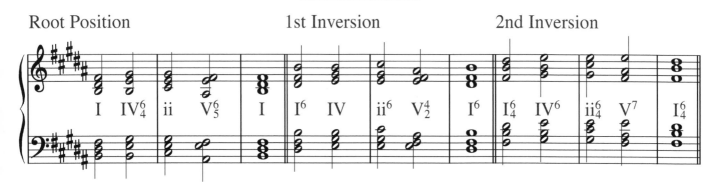

B Major

G♭ Major

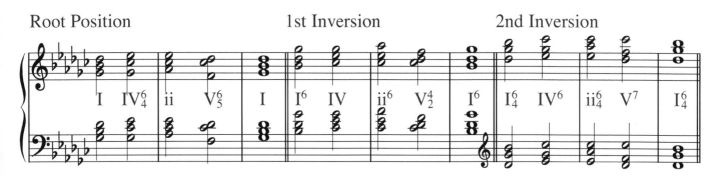

D♭ Major

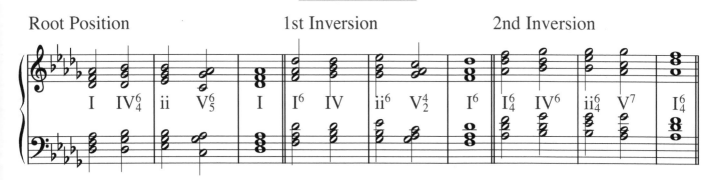

A♭ Major

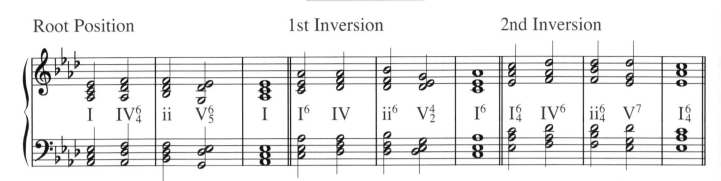

E♭ Major

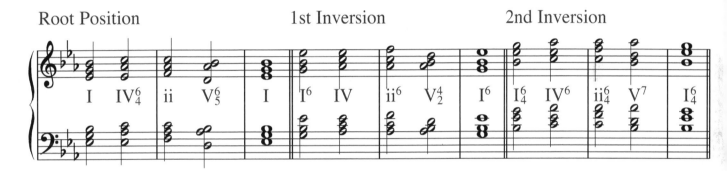

B♭ Major

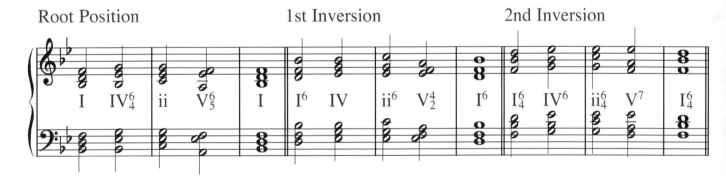

F Major

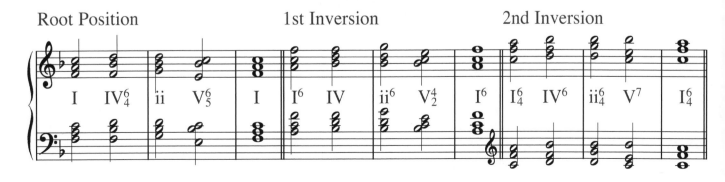

i-iv-ii°-V⁷-i Progression - All Positions

Use the A harmonic minor fingering for all keys. Practice each position separately before combining all three together in sequence.

M.M. = 92 - 108

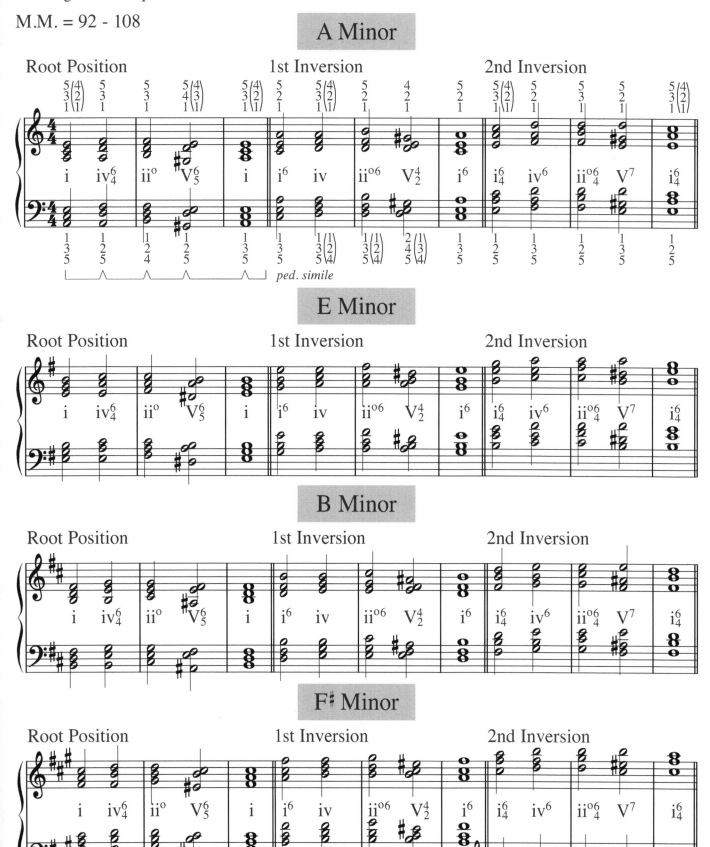

C♯ Minor

Root Position   1st Inversion   2nd Inversion

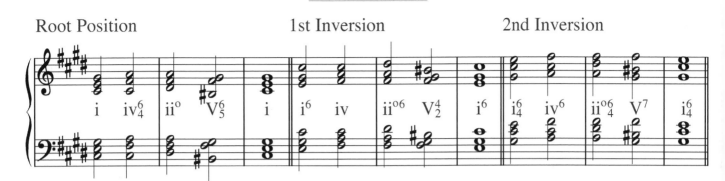

G♯ Minor

Root Position   1st Inversion   2nd Inversion

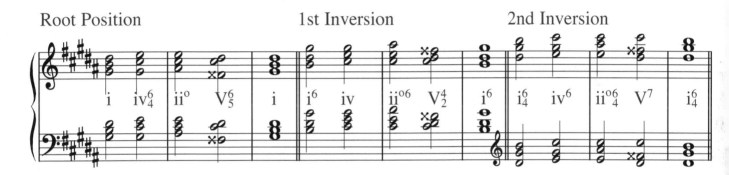

E♭ Minor

Root Position   1st Inversion   2nd Inversion

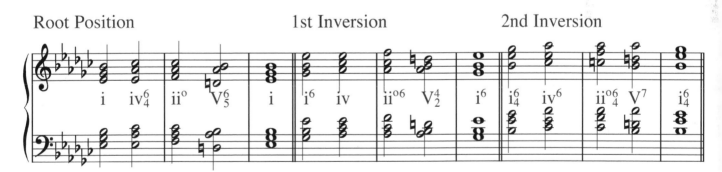

B♭ Minor

Root Position   1st Inversion   2nd Inversion

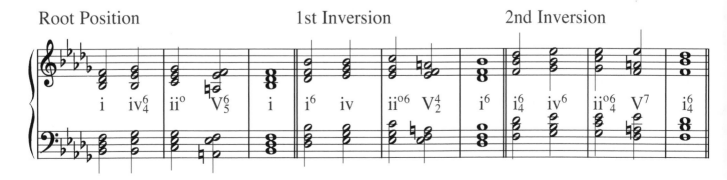

F Minor

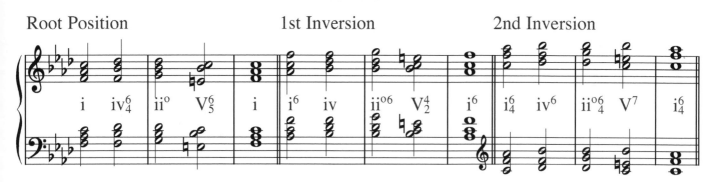

Root Position   1st Inversion   2nd Inversion

i   iv$_4^6$ ii^o V$_5^6$ i   i^6 iv   ii^{o6} V$_2^4$ i^6 i$_4^6$ iv^6 ii$_4^{o6}$ V^7 i$_4^6$

C Minor

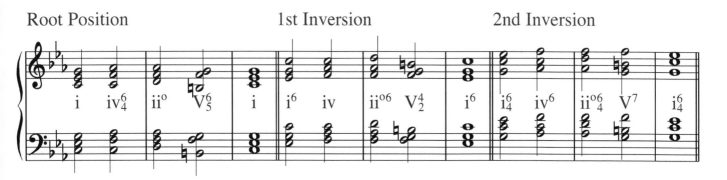

Root Position   1st Inversion   2nd Inversion

i   iv$_4^6$ ii^o V$_5^6$ i   i^6 iv   ii^{o6} V$_2^4$ i^6 i$_4^6$ iv^6 ii$_4^{o6}$ V^7 i$_4^6$

G Minor

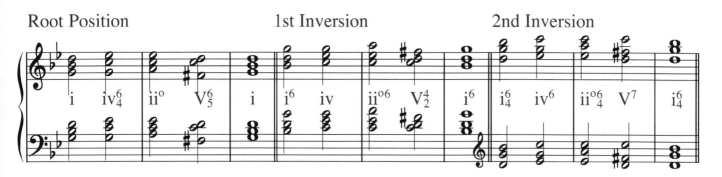

Root Position   1st Inversion   2nd Inversion

i   iv$_4^6$ ii^o V$_5^6$ i   i^6 iv   ii^{o6} V$_2^4$ i^6 i$_4^6$ iv^6 ii$_4^{o6}$ V^7 i$_4^6$

D Minor

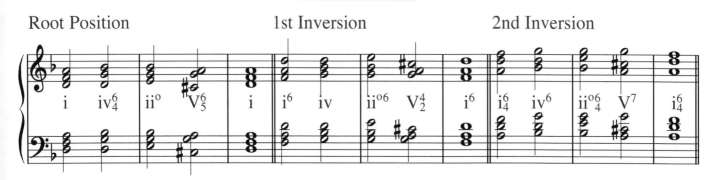

Root Position   1st Inversion   2nd Inversion

i   iv$_4^6$ ii^o V$_5^6$ i   i^6 iv   ii^{o6} V$_2^4$ i^6 i$_4^6$ iv^6 ii$_4^{o6}$ V^7 i$_4^6$

I-IV-ii-V⁷-vi Progression - All Positions

Use the C Major fingering for all keys. Practice each position separately before combining all three together in sequence.

M.M. = 92 - 108

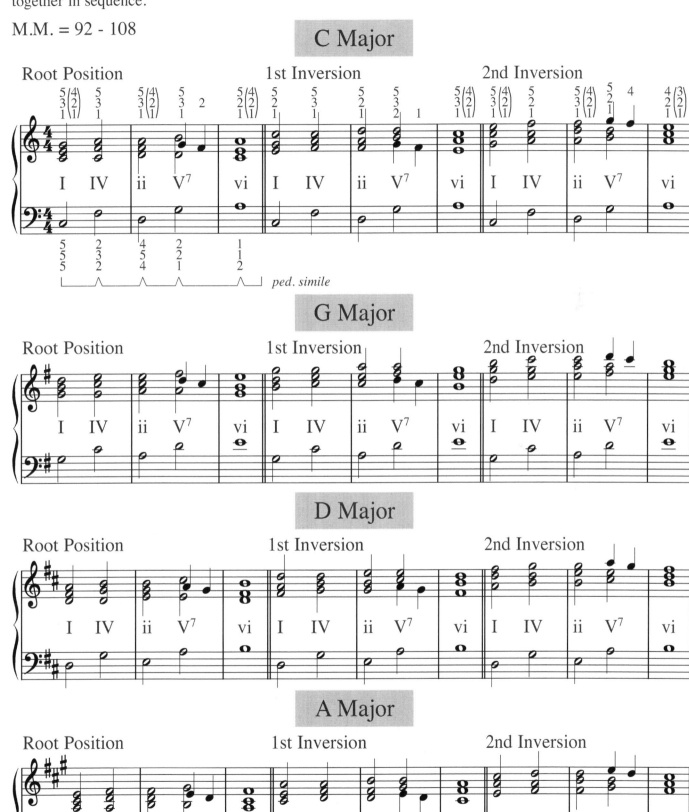

ped. simile

E Major

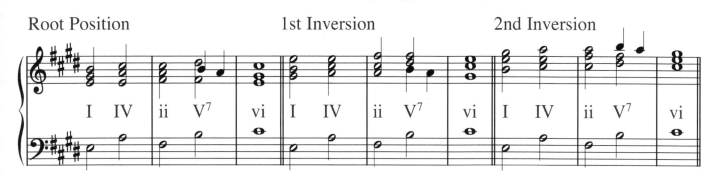

B Major

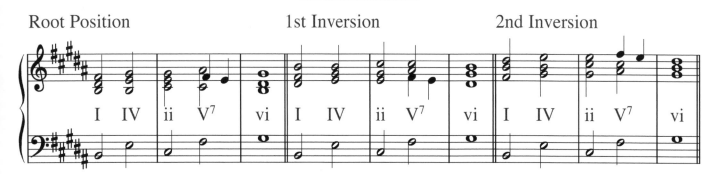

G♭ Major

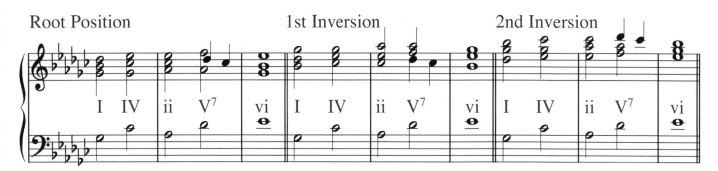

D♭ Major

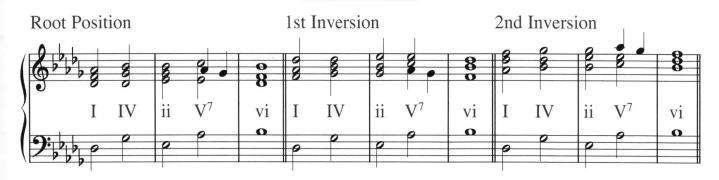

A♭ Major

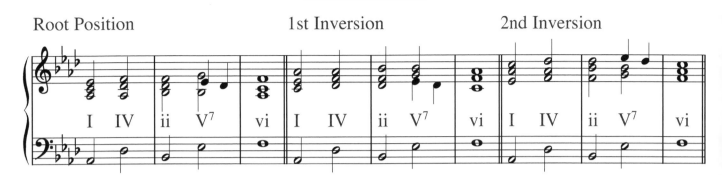

E♭ Major

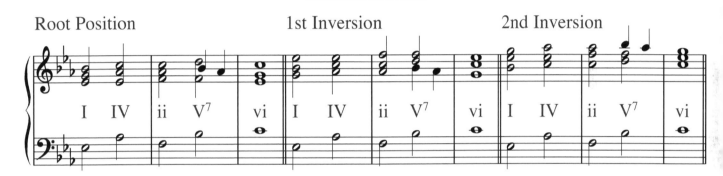

B♭ Major

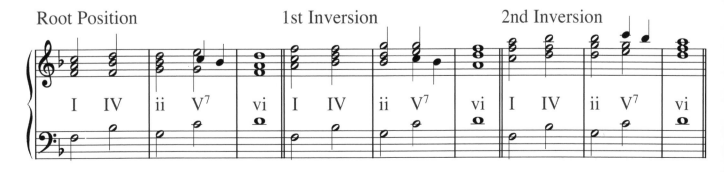

F Major

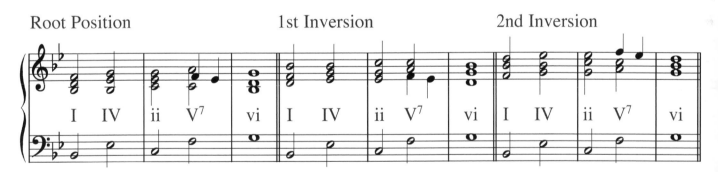

i-iv-ii°-V⁷-VI Progression - All Positions

Use the A harmonic minor fingering for all keys. Practice each position separately before combining all three together in sequence.

M.M. = 92 - 108

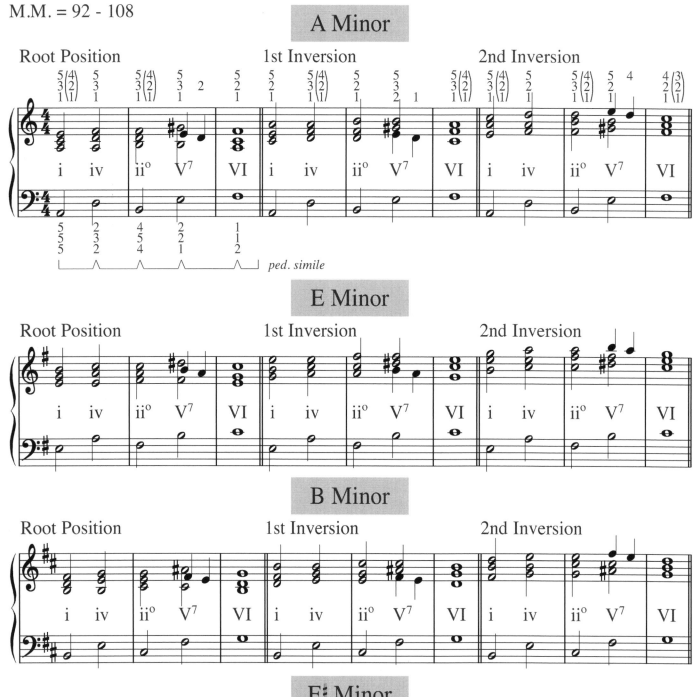

C# Minor

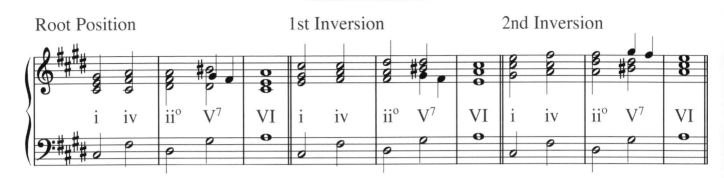

G# Minor

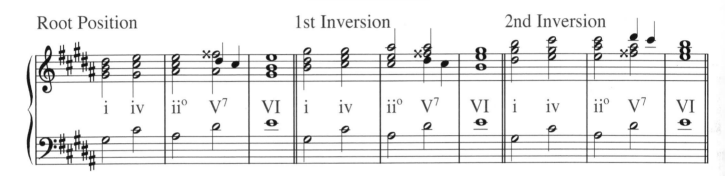

E♭ Minor

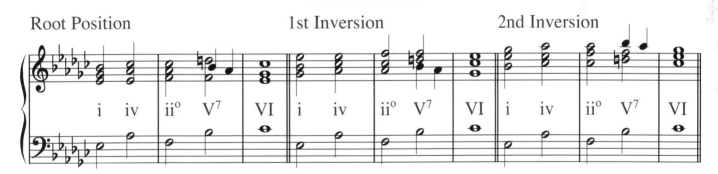

B♭ Minor

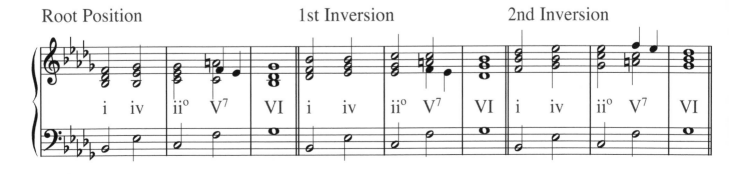

F Minor

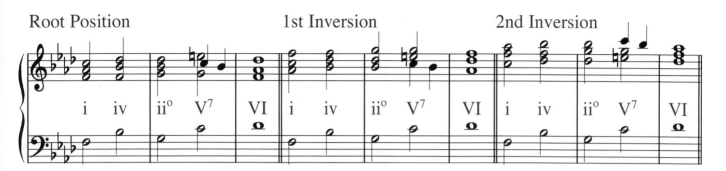

C Minor

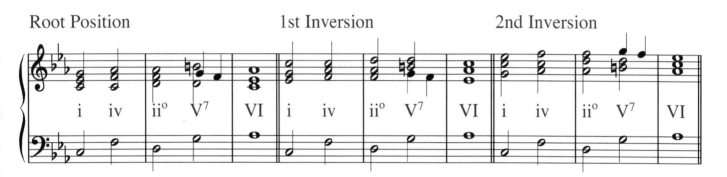

G Minor

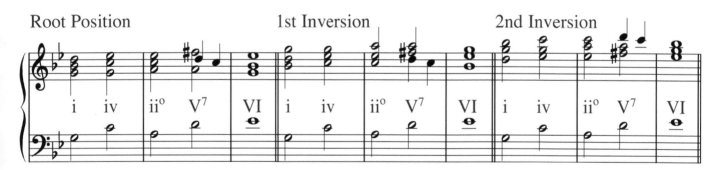

D Minor

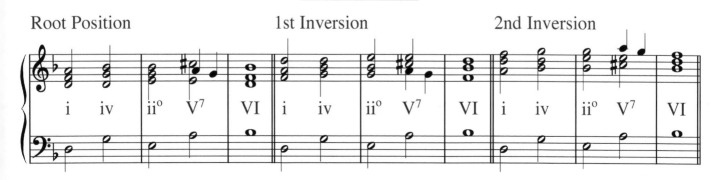

I-vi-IV-ii-I-V⁷-I Progression - All Positions

Use the C Major fingering for all keys. Practice each position separately, then in sequence. Only the major keys will be presented from this point forward. **Supplemental:** Learn the harmonic minor keys as a visual and aural exercise (i - VI - iv - ii° - i - V⁷- i).

M.M. = 92 - 108

E Major

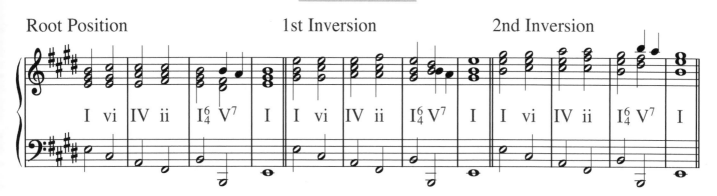

B Major

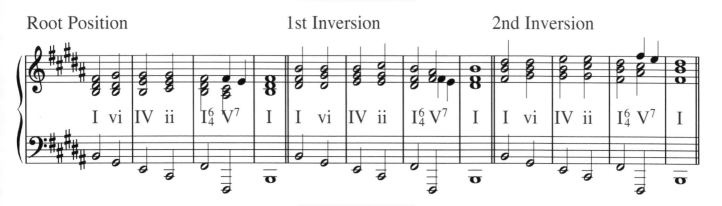

F# Major

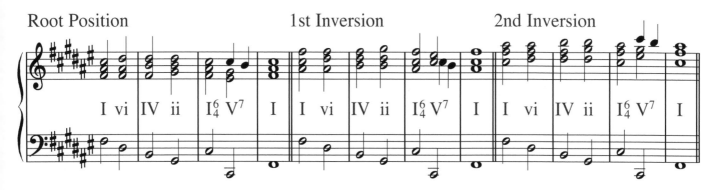

D♭ Major

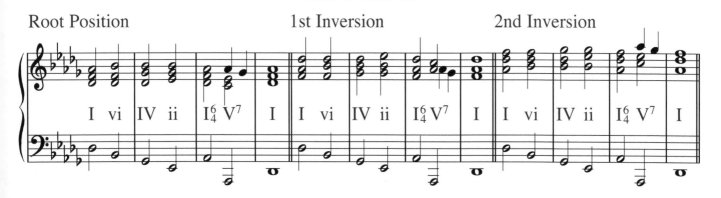

A♭ Major

E♭ Major

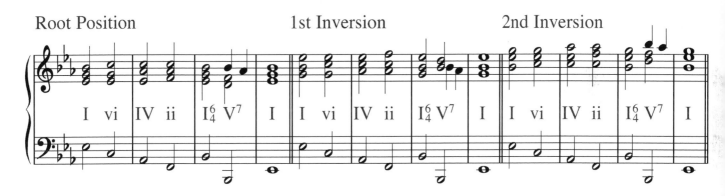

B♭ Major

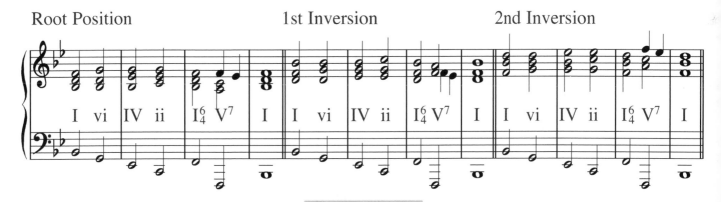

F Major

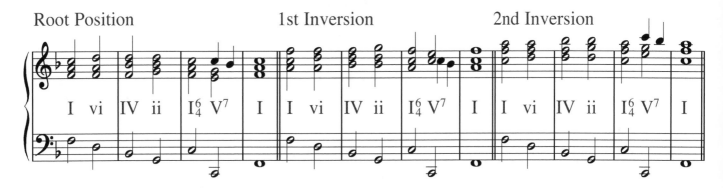

V⁷/IV Secondary Dominant Progression - All Positions

Use the C Major fingering for all keys. Practice each position separately, then in sequence.
Supplemental: Learn the harmonic minor keys as a visual and aural exercise (i - V⁷/iv - iv - V⁷- i).

M.M. = 92 - 108

C Major

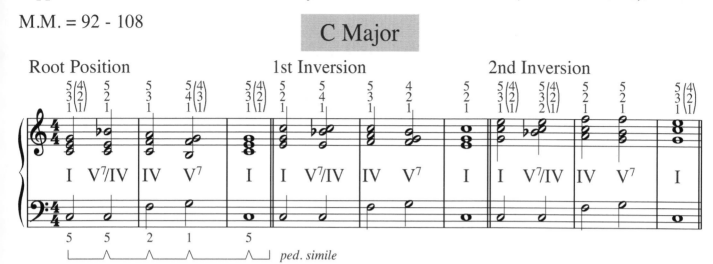

G Major

D Major

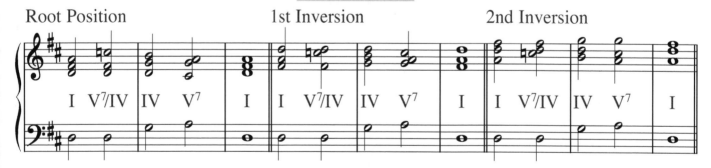

A Major

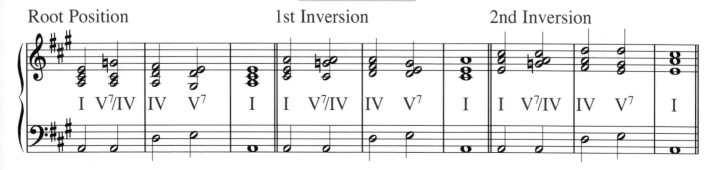

E Major

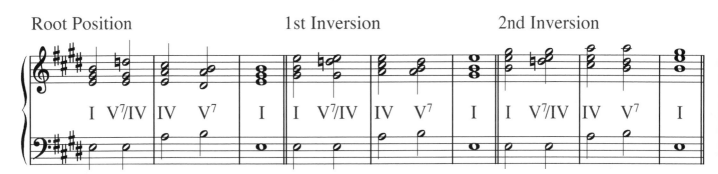

B Major

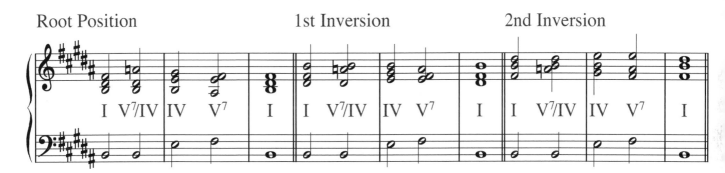

F♯ Major

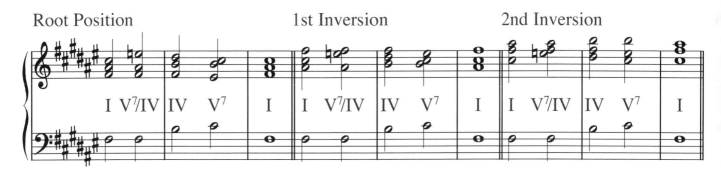

D♭ Major

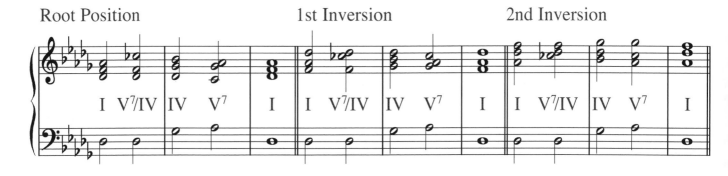

A♭ Major

Root Position   1st Inversion   2nd Inversion

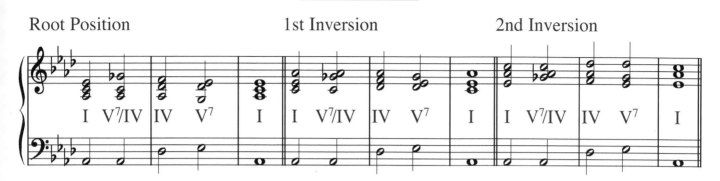

E♭ Major

Root Position   1st Inversion   2nd Inversion

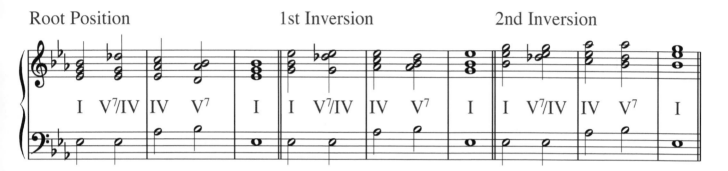

B♭ Major

Root Position   1st Inversion   2nd Inversion

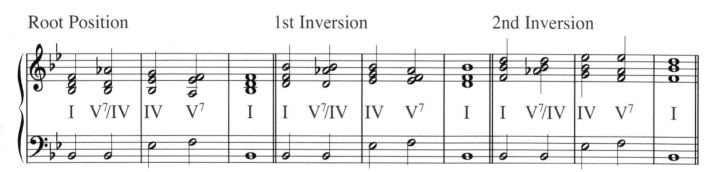

F Major

Root Position   1st Inversion   2nd Inversion

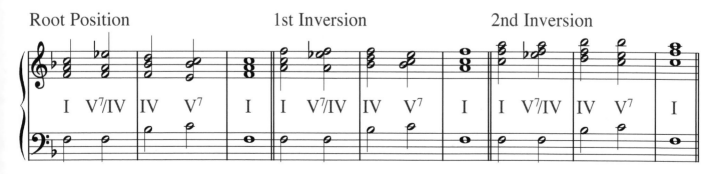

V^7/V Secondary Dominant Progression - All Positions

Use the C Major fingering for all keys. Practice each position separately, then in sequence. The harmonic minor keys are not appropriate to this progression due to the awkward ii°- V^7/V transition.

M.M. = 92 - 108

C Major

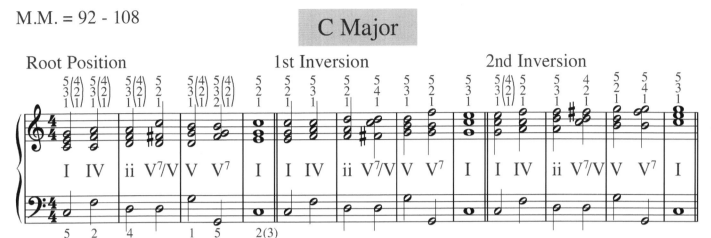

G Major

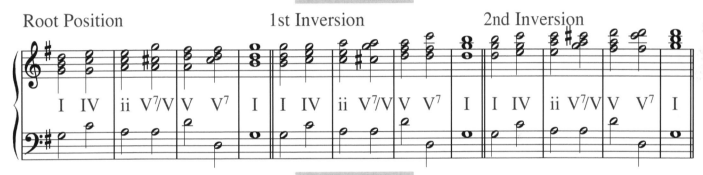

D Major

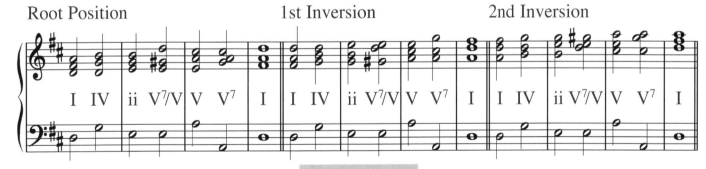

A Major

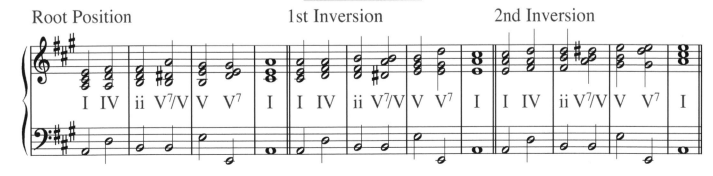

E Major

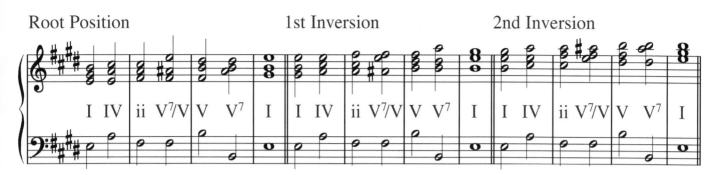

B Major

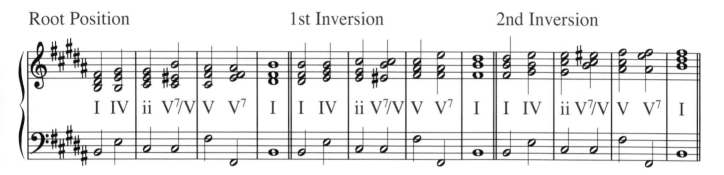

F# Major

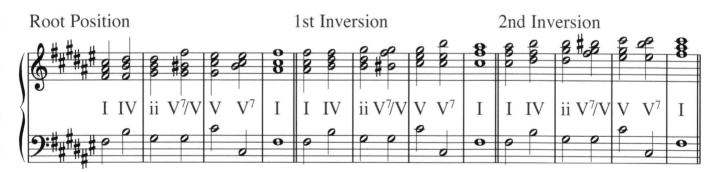

Db Major

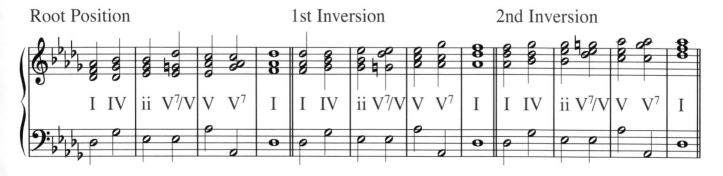

A♭ Major

Root Position   1st Inversion   2nd Inversion

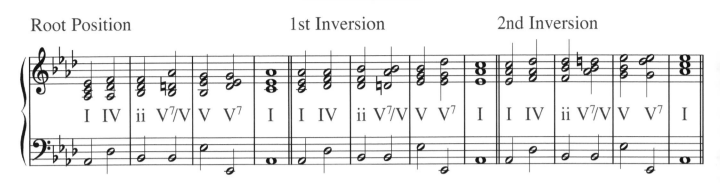

E♭ Major

Root Position   1st Inversion   2nd Inversion

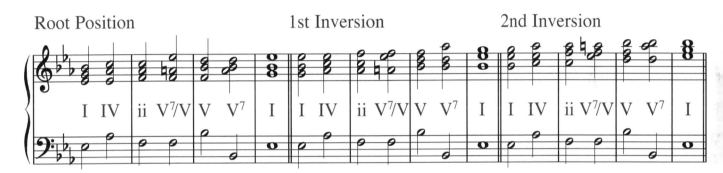

B♭ Major

Root Position   1st Inversion   2nd Inversion

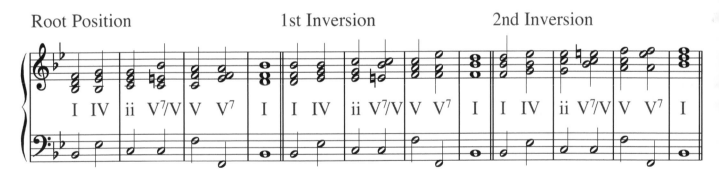

F Major

Root Position   1st Inversion   2nd Inversion

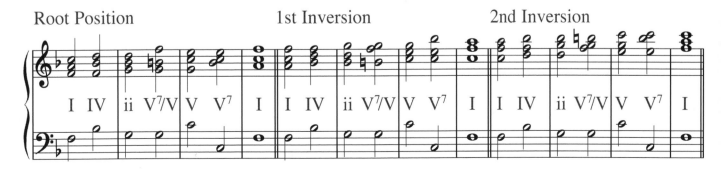

Modulation to the Dominant Progression

Use the C Major fingering for all keys. Only first inversion is presented for this progression. Having mastered the previous progressions, the student is expected to be able to determine root postion and second inversion and their appropriate fingerings, if required. **Supplemental:** Learn the harmonic minor keys as a visual and aural exercise (i - iv - V⁷- i - V⁷/V - i - ii°⁶- i⁶₄ - V⁷- i).

M.M. = 92 - 108

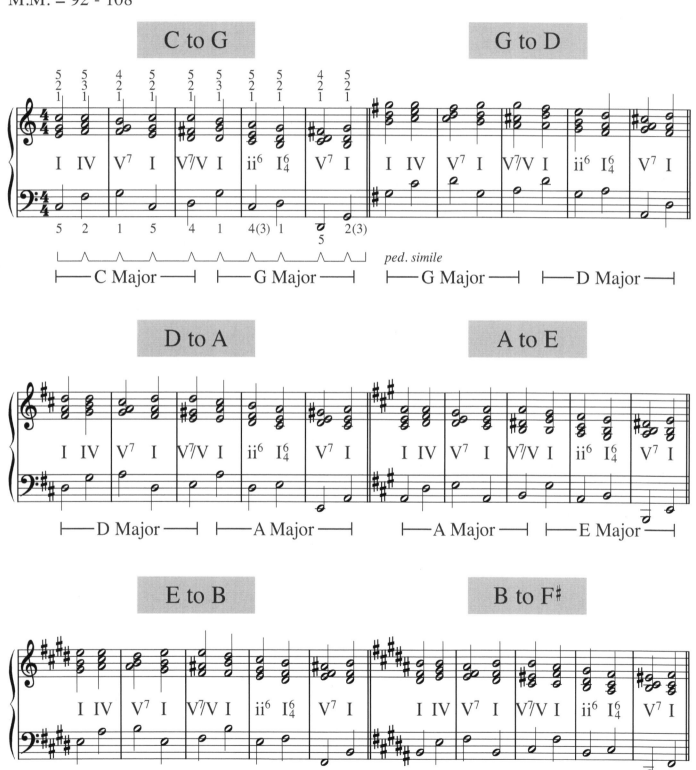

F♯ to C♯

D♭ to A♭

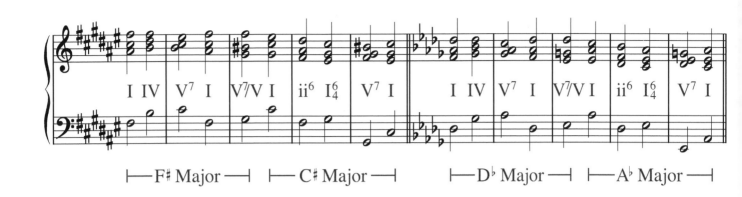

├──F♯ Major──┤ ├──C♯ Major──┤   ├──D♭ Major──┤ ├──A♭ Major──┤

A♭ to E♭

E♭ to B♭

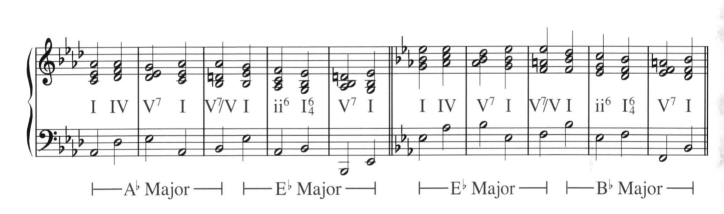

├──A♭ Major──┤ ├──E♭ Major──┤   ├──E♭ Major──┤ ├──B♭ Major──┤

B♭ to F

F to C

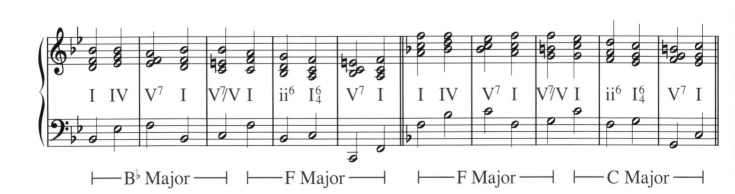

├──B♭ Major──┤ ├──F Major──┤   ├──F Major──┤ ├──C Major──┤

More Cutting-Edge Books and Products for the Music Teacher and Retailer

Piano Practice and Performance

- Designed for students and aspiring professionals.
- Four chapters present helpful and concise tips and strategies for successful practice, memorization and performance at the piano.
- Researched and tested by the authors in their own teaching practices.
- Glossary of musical terms included.
- Paperback, 68 pages.

"There is quite a degree of flexibility that acknowledges individual differences. You could quibble about the details, but the thoroughness and practicality of advice is undeniable. A very refreshing book, filling a space not occupied before in its concise format and genre."
Dr. Luiz de Moura Castro - Professor of Piano at The Hartt School, University of Hartford; international soloist and pedagogue.

Classic Series: Volume 1 Beginning Basics for the Piano

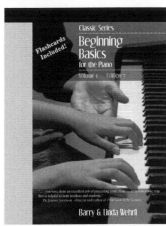

- A holistic approach for the beginning piano student, ages seven and up.
- Five workshops guide the student from learning the names of the white keys on the keyboard through playing beginner-level arrangements of famous works by Bach, Beethoven, Mozart as well as American classics.
- Posture, ear training and sight-reading projects develop skills needed to play easily and beautifully.
- Paperback, 206 pages including 12 flashcard pages.

". . . you have done an excellent job of presenting your ideas. Teachers could use your materials to enhance their teaching. It is clear that you have thought out things carefully and presented them in a systematic way that is helpful to both teachers and students."
Dr. Jeanine Jacobson - clinician and author of *Professional Piano Teaching*.

Classic Series: Volume 2 Intermediate Basics for the Piano

- A holistic approach that follows *Volume 1*, for the early-intermediate student.
- Five workshops introduce the student to subjects such as key signatures and accidentals, pedaling, ledger line notation, more complex rhythms and harmony.
- Music by classical and modern composers is arranged to demonstrate each subject, increasing in texture and complexity as the student progresses.
- Technical workouts develop strength and coordination.
- Paperback, 226 pages including 22 flashcard pages.

". . . Volume 2's five workshops cover more complicated musical concepts [than Volume 1] in a comprehensive way that will help students' positive progress. I would strongly recommend this Series to young teachers and self-study adults."
Dr. Anna Krendel - piano instructor, CAPMT District IX Coordinator.

(over)

Mastering Intervals

- For intermediate to advanced keyboardists.
- Three workshops systematically develop mastery in reading, writing and hearing any interval, enhancing composition and improvisation skills.
- 15 analyzed musical excerpts provide additional music theory insight.
- Answer Manual now included.
- Paperback, 160 pages.

"Mastering Intervals. . . [provides] a solid foundation of interval knowledge and a leg up for all musical endeavors. This in-depth workbook will be a welcome addition to any musician's library. Congratulations on a well thought out book!"
Andy LaVerne - Professor of Jazz Piano at The University of Hartford, recording artist and author of *Chord Substitutions* and *Countdown To Giant Steps.*

Music Instruction Forms: 1-Year Journal

- For all instrumentalists at any level of instruction.
- A Weekly Practice Calendar establishes the student's practice days and times and the total hours to practice within the week.
- 52 Weekly Lesson Plans carry the student through a full year's study. These easy to use plans organize assignments by category and provide spaces for the sequence, duration and grading of each assignment.
- Four Quarterly Student Progress Reports assess the student's strengths and weaknesses, quarterly. Divided into eight study categories and a general comments section, these reports keep the student on track through the year.
- Completed Journals provide a running record of the student's progress.
- Paperback, 68 pages.

Ear Training: Middle C to C

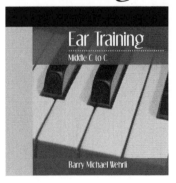

- A companion compact disc to *The Classic Series Volumes 1 and 2* or for any musician looking to improve pitch recognition.
- Develops instant pitch recognition from piano middle C to the next C above.
- Each of the 14 ear training sessions adds one new pitch at a time, providing an easy learning curve.
- A pitch is given with ample time to guess the correct key name and the answer announced afterward.
- Listen in your car, at work or at home. No teacher or assistance needed.
- Over an hour of training time on one CD.

Visit us at www.wehrlipubs.com.

Wehrli Publications

Cutting-Edge Books and Products
for the Music Teacher and Retailer

12830 Burbank Boulevard, Box 204, Valley Village, CA 91607-1402   www.wehrlipubs.com

Printed in Great Britain
by Amazon.co.uk, Ltd.,
Marston Gate.